# Overcoming Resistance to Change

self-study workbooks

# Overcoming Resistance to Change

## Russell Tobin

KOGAN
PAGE

© Copyright Russell M. Tobin 1996, 1999

First published by Fenman in 1996

Second edition published by Kogan Page in 1999

Kogan Page Limited
120 Pentonville Road
London N1 9JN, UK

Stylus Publishing Inc.
22883 Quicksilver Drive
Sterling, VA 20166, USA

---

**British Library Cataloguing in Publication Data.**
A record for this book is available from the British Library.

ISBN 0 7494 3037 0

---

Printed and bound in Great Britain by Biddles Ltd, Guildford and King's Lynn

# TABLE OF CONTENTS

# INTRODUCTION

## HOW THIS BOOK CAN HELP YOU

Change is constant, and every change, large or small, presents an opportunity for co-operation, for communication, and for great teamwork – or for the opposite.

People can resist change, unconsciously or otherwise, so this book will help you to anticipate resistance, to overcome it where it occurs, and to gain the active support of your people.

- It sets out a framework of critical steps that help you to plan for a change and then to handle the necessary discussions.

- It shows these steps being used in a range of different situations and industries, and amplifies them later.

- It helps you relate the skills described to your own situation at work.

- And it answers some of your, 'Yes, but . . .' questions.

How this book relates to others in the series is illustrated below.

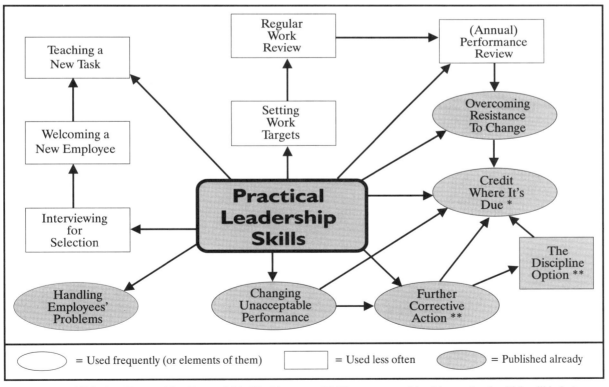

\* First published as 'Recognising Dependable Work'.    \*\* These are combined in one book which will help to avoid claims against you.

# HOW TO USE THIS BOOK

## Work Methods

You can read all this material and complete the exercises – which have a picture of a pencil in the margin, as here – in four to five hours. Or you can work through this introduction and the other sections in small chunks according to your priorities.

Always work with a pen or pencil in your hand and use the panel on the right for your own notes and comments.

The exercises, and the author's comments on them, help you to examine ideas, and to look at your own work situation from a fresh viewpoint. If any questions make you feel uncertain then ask for help; some sources of help are shown opposite.

You will notice from the Table of Contents that the book is organized to help you dip into different areas of interest as you wish. So keep it handy for whenever you have a problem connected with bringing in change.

There is a whole section on trying out the skills, so use every opportunity you can to put the tips into practice. Experiment, get feedback, persevere.

This book is best read after the one on *Practical Leadership Skills* which is the foundation for the whole series of books. If you haven't read it, and if you want to deal quickly with a change situation or a presentation, then go right ahead with this book. But try to read the foundation book later.

Be warned. The skills outlined here are not second nature, they have to be worked at.

# WHAT SUPPORT IS AVAILABLE?

If you are working through this book as one part of a development programme, or on your own initiative, there are several people who can help you.

YOUR BOSS    Who wants you to succeed. S/he may also be your COACH, especially with regard to the items marked with an asterisk (*) in the Table of Contents. If your boss would like a quick refresher on coaching then 'A page for the boss' in the book on *Practical Leadership Skills* provides just that.

COLLEAGUES    Who want members of their team to be effective. They also know that if they give help to you they can request help from you later.

YOUR STAFF    Who also have a vested interest in your being effective. Because they see you as no one else does you can ask them to give you objective feedback.

YOUR MENTOR    If you have a separate mentor, or tutor, that person is there specifically to help you to succeed.

THE AUTHOR    Who offers further books, shown on page 1, which help with the all-the-time skills needed for *practical leadership* and with *specific and important discussions*. These specific books demonstrate the Practical Leadership Skills being applied in a range of situations.

He also runs workshops for you to develop and check out your skills, and to receive feedback and advice. Telephone **01280 817918**.

If the first three know what you are doing – and you may need to tell them – they can help.  So why not enlist their support?  Mutual support is good teamwork.

## Notes

So that you give some time to this question of support why not take a minute to note the names of people whom you could approach for help?  You may wish to discuss some of the questions in this book or ask about their experiences.

Whom can you talk with?  Who else may be working through this book? Or in learning mode with other things?

_____

_____

_____

_____

_____

_____

_____

_____

# WHY DO PEOPLE RESIST CHANGE?

Try asking your fellow managers or team leaders the question, 'Why do people at work resist change, unconsciously or even deliberately?' Ask yourself the same question. Then please note the answers below; they will be useful to you later on.

Write down your own ideas BEFORE you turn the page please. There is one idea already to start you off.

'Why do people at work resist change, unconsciously or even deliberately?'

It could mean more work for them.

# Comments

If you and your colleagues answered that question as hundreds of others have done, your ideas will probably include some of the following:

| |
|---|
| • *It could mean more work for them.* |
| • *They don't believe the reason given for the change. (They don't trust the organization or its managers.)* |
| • *There have been failures in the past. (Management didn't think it through properly.)* |
| • *They could lose money, eg overtime, or other perks.* |
| • *They may have to work with new people and this can be difficult.* |
| • *There will be new things to learn. (Harder for older people??).* |
| • *They ask, 'What's wrong with the present way? (We've been doing it this way all our working lives.)'* |
| • *They don't understand the reason for change.* |
| • *They ask, 'Could we work ourselves out of a job?'* |
| • *People are comfortable in a rut. (There is fear of the unknown.)* |
| • *They say, 'It won't work, it's been tried before.'* |
| • *They can see too many problems with the change.* |
| • *They believe they will lose out in some way or another.* |
| • *The change has not been well explained.* |
| • *'Management may ask what you think but they don't take any notice.'* |

Most managers would give answers such as these but an interesting thing happens when the question is posed from a different direction; see the next page.

## Resistance is legitimate

If you asked the same managers or team leaders why *they themselves* are sometimes slow to implement change they come up with very similar reasons, often using the same words. What they are really saying is that their reasons for resisting change are the same as those which they see in their staff. Try it for yourself.

Why are YOU sometimes slow or reluctant to just leap into action and do what the boss wants straightaway?

Now compare your answers with those on the previous pages.

When you look at both sets of reasons you can acknowledge that resistance to change is understandable and, indeed, legitimate (refusal is something different and we'll deal with that later). So it makes sense to anticipate resistance and to plan to overcome it.

## WHAT DOES 'CHANGE' MEAN?

It can be as simple as asking Jack to cover Jill's job for a short time. Or as complicated as moving to a new building, or closing part of the business or starting a new venture.

In this book we are *not* dealing with situations where people are failing to meet a defined standard which is already required of them.[1]

If the standard is raised, however, that is a change. Increasing output or improving quality are examples where people have been performing acceptably to current standards but those standards now have to be raised.

With change you are asking people to do something which may be completely new to them. Or something which they know of but have no deep understanding about.

Some employees may co-operate eagerly because they are keen to develop new skills and knowledge, or they feel safe in their jobs, or have confidence in the organization. Others may react less well because of their experience, the attitudes of their work group, their vested interests, etc.

The first type of person should not be taken for granted and the second should not be allowed to effectively veto change.

Most people will fall between the two extremes. They are probably happy with things as they are, they worry about their new workload and their ability to learn (as *they* perceive these things). They may worry about the perceived risk of problems or failure (and how they believe their boss will react), and so on.

So, given that resistance to change is understandable and even legitimate, how do you improve your chances of success? One answer lies in using a sensible method, or framework, for planning and introducing changes, large or small: a framework which also helps employees to participate in a meaningful way.

> Learning new things can be just as hard for a 22-year-old as it is for a 62-year-old. In fact, young people can be much more narrow in their outlook and experience.

---

[1] When people are not performing to a well-established standard you probably need the book on *Changing Unacceptable Performance*.

## IS CHANGE REALLY NEEDED?

Making routine changes may not carry much risk. For example:

- asking one competent person to cover for another who is visiting the dentist

- giving regular instructions about the job, eg what the priorities for the day are

- replacing a piece of machinery for maintenance, and so on.

However, with bigger non-routine changes the opportunities for errors and resistance naturally increase (and even small changes may carry some risk). For each such change you should consider the following questions:

- Can you be specific about what is making you unhappy with the present situation?

- Is it your business anyway?

- What will you do if you meet resistance?

- What would happen if you ignored the problem?

- Is the likely gain worth the potential trouble?

- *Why* is it important to make the change?

Unless you properly analyse the problem and are clear what you want from the change you could just be creating more problems for yourself – and for others.

## Question

Have you ever, ever, gone into a change and later wished you had thought it through better? Circle one below.

### YES　　NO

Whether a change is large or small you still have to gain commitment to it. Unless you work for success you risk failure. Why take the risk? Use the 'framework' that follows to improve your chances of success.

# THE FRAMEWORK OF CRITICAL STEPS

for

## OVERCOMING RESISTANCE TO CHANGE

**(Consider objective, implications, alternatives and discretion.)**

This is the planning stage *before* the discussion.
It varies depending on the scale of the change.

1. **Explain the conditions which have brought about the need for change.**

   Set the scene with important information so the employee can understand the reason for the change.

2. **Explain the detail of the change and how it will affect the employee.**

   Say what the employee must do, how they will gain or lose. Anticipate questions and give the answers now.

3. **If applicable, include a practical demonstration or teach the employee how to carry out the new process.**

   Use anything, anything at all, that will help the employee to understand and learn what is needed.

4. **Ask the employee how he feels about the proposals; identify his major hang-ups and recognize any new problems.**

   This step is a safety net for the problems you did not anticipate. Listen actively and note concerns. Don't let problems pressure you. Check you understand them.

5. **Ask for his suggestions for (a) overcoming the problems and (b) implementing the change, using a joint problem-solving approach.**

   Having decided to what extent you will stay with your original objective, you switch from finding problems to solving them with help from the employee. Move forward to action and take the employee with you.

> Where you read 'he' or 'his', as in Steps 4 & 5 here, will you please include 'or she'. This is to avoid clumsy language and no discrimination, prejudice or bias is intended.

These steps will be explained in more detail later.

---

## WHY A 'FRAMEWORK'?

You probably use checklists in your job already. This framework of critical behaviour steps is one more; you use it in your own way according to the employee and the situation.

## Are the steps *really* critical?

The sequence is important and the words have been carefully chosen. So if you miss a step, or go out of sequence, this makes success more difficult. You don't have to follow the framework slavishly but if you miss a step or get out of sequence be aware of this and be ready to re-enter the framework where you left off, even starting again.

A well-structured discussion saves time, avoids misunderstandings, reduces stress, and lowers the risk of failure. If you follow these steps you will be more in control of yourself, and of the situation, as your actions influence the other person's reactions. Even if you do not reach a solution at once you will probably have done as well as possible.

## TEAMWORK AND PRESENTATIONS

You can use this framework when your team is making a presentation. Thus one member could handle Step 1 and another Step 2. A third could handle Step 3, using visual aids as the others speak. Another could handle Step 4, labelling and listing any major hang-ups or new problems as they arise. The team leader could work with the audience on 5(a). Another member then moves them from 5(a) to 5(b) and thence to a follow-up date.

## Question

In what circumstances may you and members of a team come together to make a presentation? See if you can come up with at least two ideas, even if your team is only you and one other.

---

# THE PRACTICAL LEADERSHIP SKILLS FRAMEWORK

The framework of seven, all-the-time Practical Leadership Skills is always in the background. Here you can see how it shapes the framework for Overcoming Resistance to Change.

## 1. Maintain or enhance the self-esteem of the employee.

Being given full information will enhance their self-esteem: they are not being taken for granted and they can actively participate.

## 2. Don't attack the person, FOCUS ON THE PROBLEM.

You focus first on the need for change. Next, on the problems this means for the employee. Then on the problems that the employee sees. Next, on overcoming these. Finally, on the problem of implementation.

## 3. Don't assume that the employee has committed an offence.

Don't mistake reluctance for deliberate obstruction (we know that resistance is legitimate).

## 4. Encourage the employee to express their opinions and make suggestions.

The Change framework is designed to encourage opinions and suggestions – to gain participation and commitment.

## 5. Allow the employee adequate time to think through the problem and suggest a solution.

Time to accept the idea of a change is important. Given time, employees nearest to the change are often in the best position to think of solutions.

## 6. Ensure that the employee has an appropriate ACTION programme.

An appropriate action programme could be for the employee to think about the problems, or give the change a go, or it could be a series of programmed steps.

## 7. Always set a specific follow-up date.

This lets you discuss new problems, review progress, and congratulate the employee on success so far.

If you have not read the book, *Practical Leadership Skills* try to do so soon.

# DEMONSTRATIONS

## INTRODUCTION

There are six examples of different bosses using the framework for Overcoming Resistance to Change, plus the framework of Practical Leadership Skills, in their own different ways. The demonstrations are applicable to a wide range of situations and industries.

With each demonstration you'll find comments on what the boss is doing as s/he follows the framework. After each one you will be asked to check the boss's performance against the framework for Practical Leadership Skills (the PLS) because the specific framework for Overcoming Resistance to Change is simply a sequence for going through the PLS.

You will later be asked to consider how the demonstrated discussions might compare with situations in your own work place, so please think about that as you read through them.

After studying the demonstrations and further explanation of the steps (later) you may find yourself saying, "Yes, but what if there are other problems?" or "What about . . . ?" and so on. Most of your questions should be answered in the section on Exceptional Situations.

# 1. A PROBLEM WITH TAX RECEIPTS

Here a Sales Manager, Adrian, is having a regular meeting with one of his three Sales Engineers. This is Simon, who works mainly in the capital and uses taxis quite a lot. The need for change will become clear during step 1 on the next page.

---

(Consider objective, implications, alternatives and discretion.)

---

Adrian's objective in the discussion is to get an immediate action plan that will work, but he will still have a follow-up date to review its success.

One implication of the change is some inconvenience for Simon and thus some resistance.

Adrian has no alternative for the overall objective he must achieve, and little discretion over timing.

NB     The comments on the right of the dialogue explain how the boss is using the critical steps. Please read the demonstration with a pencil in your hand to mark the text.

For a better understanding of the critical steps read the section, 'The Critical Steps Explained Further'.

✓

| DIALOGUE | COMMENTS |
|---|---|
| **1. Explain the conditions which have brought about the need for change.** | |
| Adrian: 'Simon, I've had finance on to me about tax receipts.' | *Indicating the topic of conversation.* |
| Simon: 'Oh yes, what do they want?' | |
| Adrian: 'Well, the tax people are getting awkward about the tax that we claim back on expenses without providing receipts . . .' | *Setting the scene.* |
| Simon: 'That's right, you can't get receipts for everything, I wish we could.' | |
| Adrian: 'Anyway the taxman is saying that if we don't provide more receipts, we're going to lose the tax that we claim back and the thing is, for the company as a whole, that's a good few thousand in a year.' | *Describing the problem and an overpowering need for change.* |
| Simon: 'Well my share doesn't come to much, I can tell you.' | |
| **2. Explain the detail of the change and how it will affect the employee.** | |
| Adrian: 'Well, what it means for you Simon is this. Like all the engineers, your main expenses are travel, food and drink.' | *Going from the general to the particular.* |
| Simon: 'Well, there's a few other things.' | |
| Adrian: 'Yes, okay. And what I'm asking you, and all the others, to do, as from now, is make sure that you get receipts for taxis and for food and drink. Those are the main problem areas.' | *Shows that Simon is not the only one affected.* |
| Simon: 'What about public transport?' | |
| Adrian: 'There's no tax on those, Simon, so they're not worried.' | *This is one of the implications that Adrian checked before speaking to Simon.* |
| Simon: 'Oh.' | |

✓

| | |
|---|---|
| 3. If applicable, include a practical demonstration or teach the employee how to carry out the new process. | *Not applicable. Simon should not need to learn how to get receipts.* |

| | |
|---|---|
| 4. Ask the employee how he feels about the proposals: identify his major hang-ups and recognize any new problems. | |

Adrian: 'So if you can all manage that we should be okay; can you see any problems?'

*Deliberately asks the question even though problems are hard to imagine.*

Simon: 'Well, you've not been in a city taxi for a while have you?'

Adrian: 'What do you mean?'

*Seeking clarification.*

Simon: 'Well, can you imagine? You're standing on the pavement asking for a receipt and there's a new passenger in a hurry; what do you think the driver's going to say?'

Adrian: 'Yes, I can imagine. What about meals and drinks?'

*Not arguing; empathizing without agreeing. Leaves the problem for solving in the next step. Asks for any more problems.*

Simon: 'Well, that's why we don't get receipts now, isn't it? I mean, at lunchtime every place is heaving. You know what they'd say, 'In a minute,' and that's as far as you'll get.'

Adrian: 'Well, I know what you mean, I do indeed, but . . .'

*Not denying the difficulty. Sees no reason to stay in this step any longer and decides to move forward with the original proposal.*

| | |
|---|---|
| 5. Ask for his suggestions for <br><br> (a) overcoming the problems | |

Adrian: '. . . we can't afford to lose something like ten thousand a year, it takes a lot of sales to get that back.'

*Re-emphasizes the need for change so as to show determination and switch from problem-finding to problem-solving.*

Simon: 'Uhmm.'

Adrian: 'So what's the best way of dealing with the taxi driver do you think?'

*Uses an open question, a coaching question to get Simon to focus on this one problem.*

Simon: 'I dunno. I don't want to deal with an irate taxi driver, Adrian.'

Adrian: 'Well, what I do Simon is, when the driver says 'Four fifty', I work out the tip, and say, 'Will you give me a receipt for five eighty?' They've never said no yet and if they did I'd just say 'Right, take four fifty then.'

*Adrian **could** have said, 'Well, you've got to, so what's the best way?' But as he is creating this problem for Simon he is happy to put in his own idea as part of joint problem-solving*

Simon: 'Yes, I see what you mean. But food and drink's not the same is it?'

Adrian: 'I agree, but they want you coming back don't they?'

*If Simon had not accepted that idea Adrian would have asked again for Simon's ideas.*

*Adrian follows the theme of 'What's in it for them to do what you want.'*

Simon: 'I suppose so.'

Adrian: 'So how can you handle them then?'

*A coaching question. He wants to avoid telling Simon how to go about it.*

Silence

Simon: 'Well, if it's busy when you go in they're not interested . . . '

*Silence keeps Simon thinking without pushing or attacking him.*

Adrian: 'When you go in, yes?'

*Agreeing and prompting for the next thought.*

Simon: 'I suppose, I'll just have to ask when I'm leaving; I need a receipt.'

Adrian: 'Yes, they're used to it. And if you do ask earlier they'll have time to make it out and you needn't hang around when you leave.'

*Building on Simon's idea.*

Simon: 'Yes, right.'

> and   b) implementing the change,
>
>    using a joint problem-solving approach.

Adrian: 'Okay. Any other ideas, Simon, for making it happen, I mean?'

*Another coaching question focusing on (b) implementing the change.*

Simon: 'No, I don't think so, if we've got to have them, I'll fix it.'

Adrian: 'Okay, from now on then?'

Simon: 'Okay.'

Continued overleaf

Adrian: 'Now, next Wednesday, Simon, instead of dropping your expenses in my tray can we make a point of talking through them? And we'll see if you've had problems with anything else?'

Simon: 'Okay.'

Adrian: 'Right, thanks very much Simon. What's next?'

*The follow-up date is to ensure it happens. Without that Simon may think this is just one of those things that the boss doesn't really care about.*

*Adrian also wants to be able to confirm that all has gone well.*

*Having set a follow-up date they can now move to something else.*

## Why not just send out a memo?

When a change is as simple as this one, and when it is something that *has* to happen, you may wonder why the boss should not just send out a memo. He could do, of course, but sometimes people are slow to read memos they don't like.

This short discussion took place during a regular meeting and at the end of it the boss, Adrian, had worked with Simon to overcome any problems.

Three such discussions (Adrian has three Sales Engineers) would take about nine minutes in all. Not a lot.

Against that, how long would it take to compose a memorandum that anticipated *all* the possible objections *and also* dealt with them? What length would such a memo need to be and what would be its effect?

See the next page for a check on the framework for Practical Leadership Skills.

That discussion on tax receipts took about three minutes – without reading the comments. Check it against the framework for

## PRACTICAL LEADERSHIP SKILLS.

See if you agree that the boss applied all seven of the all-the-time skills.

---

1. **Maintain or enhance the self-esteem of the employee.**

   The boss has involved the employee in solving a problem of concern to the company. Also, Simon can see his way through the problems he will have.

2. **Don't attack the person,**
   **FOCUS ON THE PROBLEM.**

   No attacking. The boss focused first on the money that could be lost to the company. Then on the employee's problems as the employee saw them.

3. **Don't assume that the employee has committed an offence.**

   The boss could have thought the employee was being deliberately obstructive, but didn't.

4. **Encourage the employee to express his opinions and make suggestions.**

   Yes, to both opinions and suggestions.

5. **Allow the employee adequate time to think through the problem and to suggest a solution.**

   On the taxi problem the boss was able to make a suggestion from his own experience for the employee to agree with (the joint problem-solving approach). When the boss stayed quiet the employee thought of asking for a meal receipt .

6. **Ensure that the employee has an appropriate ACTION programme.**

   Yes, concerning taxis, meals and drinks; he will 'fix it' - and he knows how.

7. **Always set a specific follow-up date.**

   Yes, and checking for any new problems shows Adrian's wish to have it right.

---

# Notes

# 2. GOING ON A TRAINING COURSE

The manager here is Jenny. She has been following up on the the results of performance review discussions with several of her junior managers. She is now talking to Melvin, who is one of them.

> (Consider objective, implications, alternatives and discretion.)

The objective overall is performance improvement, together with personal development, for her managers. For Melvin the objective will become clear in the discussion. The objective of the discussion itself is to get Melvin moving in the right direction.

One implication is that Melvin will be somewhat reluctant, plus considerations regarding staying away from home, and about expenses.

Jenny does not know of any alternatives to her proposal for attendance on a training course, she has looked at the question of open learning but, at this time, there was little effective material available.

There is discretion over timing and over the best way of achieving the objective so Jenny is open to better ideas.

NB    The comments on the right of the dialogue explain how the boss is using the critical steps. Please read the demonstration with a pencil in your hand to mark the text.

For a better understanding of the critical steps read the section, 'The Critical Steps Explained Further'.

| DIALOGUE | COMMENTS |
|---|---|
| **1. Explain the conditions which have brought about the need for change.** | |
| Jenny: 'Melvin, I've got some good news and some good news.' | *A non-threatening start.* |
| Melvin: 'Well, that's a nice change.' | |
| Jenny: 'Well, I want to pick up on your performance review and then I've got an idea I'd like to try out with you.' | *Announcing the subject. And, 'I've got an idea', shows she is open to other ideas.* |
| Melvin: 'Okay.' | |
| Jenny: 'You remember that you got mostly good work results but we shared some concern over a couple of missed deadlines?' | *Going over common ground in order to lay the foundation for her proposal.* |
| Melvin: 'Yes.' | |
| Jenny: 'And that was linked with you taking on too much work.' | |
| Melvin: 'I think that's not so bad now.' | *An honest opinion.* |
| Jenny: 'But still not absolutely right, eh?' | *She would have needed good evidence to argue with Melvin, but it is not necessary.* |
| Melvin: 'No, not yet.' | |
| Jenny: 'And then there was the question of communication skills linked with how hard it is, sometimes, to get co-operation from other departments?' | *Jenny is reading from her copy of the Performance review form which Melvin had agreed.* |
| Melvin: 'You can say that again.' | |
| Jenny: 'Anyway, it was important enough for us to agree that I'd look out for something that could help you.' | |
| Melvin: 'Yes, I remember.' | |
| **2. Explain the detail of the change and how it will affect the employee.** | |

Continued on next page

✓

> 2.  Explain the detail of the change and how it will affect the employee.

| | | |
|---|---|---|
| Jenny: | 'Now what I've got is something that will help you with the communication skills, with the workload problem and with getting co-operation. And with your overall development.' | *Doing a selling job.* |
| Melvin: | 'Sounds too good to be true.' | |
| Jenny: | 'Well, I looked up the notes for a course that I did myself, a few years back, before I came here, and I rang the company that ran it and they still do it.' | *Introducing the idea of a course and endorsing it at the same time.* |
| Melvin: | 'Hmm, hmm.' | |
| Jenny: | 'Anyway, the upshot is that I've got you booked on a three day workshop for 16 to 18 May. That's well before your own holiday and there's no one else in your section away at that time.' | *Showing that she has looked at some of the implications.* |
| Melvin: | 'Three days?' | |
| Jenny: | 'Yes, it'll mean an early start on day one, to get there for 9.30, but then you'll have two nights in a four star hotel with all expenses paid.' | *A small minus point then two pluses to sell the idea.* |
| Melvin: | 'So I've got to be away from home, have I?' | |
| Jenny: | 'I'm afraid so, Melvin. The hotel is in a place called Brackley, on the A43, so it's going to be a two hour drive, and there's no way I can ask you to spend four hours a day on the road.' | *Jenny does not take that as a major hang-up, just as a question. Continues with the detail and shows further consideration for Melvin.* |
| Melvin: | 'Hmm' | |
| Jenny: | 'Now, on the last day you should be finished by four o'clock so you'll be home in reasonable time.' | *Another selling point to offset the staying away from home and the early start on day 1.* |
| Melvin: | 'I see.' | |
| Jenny: | 'The course itself is excellent, I remember it did me a lot of good, and you'll be there with about five other guys from different organizations who want to make the same sort of improvements as you do. | *Showing the course is not unknown and that Melvin is not the only one attending.* |

Melvin: 'Hmmm.'

Jenny: So you could make some useful contacts and you'll have some company in the evenings, if you want.'

Melvin: 'I see, what about expenses?'

*More plus points.*

| 3. | If applicable, include a practical demonstration or teach the employee how to carry out the new process. |
|----|---|

Jenny: 'Right. Before we go into that, let me give you two things. This is a brochure about the hotel, shows you where it is and what it's got, and this is a set of joining instructions that tells you about the course itself. You can look at those later, but the objectives are dead right.'

Melvin: 'Okay.'

*Jenny defers questions. She uses two visual aids to help him to understand what is involved.*

*Seeing the Performance Review form used by Jenny also helped his understanding.*

| 4. | Ask the employee how he feels about the proposals: identify his major hang-ups and recognize any new problems. |
|----|---|

Jenny: 'Now, anything you want to ask about – besides expenses?'

Melvin: 'Well, what about expenses?'

Jenny: 'Well, there's no way we want you to be out of pocket, so the mileage allowance is the same as you get paid for other journeys.'

Melvin: 'Okay.'

Jenny: 'And the rest of it? Dinner and wine is arranged. The hotel bill is paid. Drinks and phone calls are separate for you to pay and claim back.'

Melvin: 'Hmm, right. Fair enough.'

Jenny: 'Anything else, Melvin?'

*Now that she has finished giving information she can switch to working at listening.*

*An easy answer, she had assumed Melvin would take this for granted.*

*Jenny could have mentioned these in Step 2 but this step is a safety net for the things she over-looked.*

*She wants to deal with all potential problems in one go – if she can.*

Melvin: 'What about my work? I appreciate my staff will be here but being away does leave a bit of a hole.'

Jenny: 'True enough. What aspect of your work are you thinking of?'

*A nice open question, but probing.*

Melvin: 'Well, there's always some emergencies. And I'll find a desk full of stuff when I get back.'

Jenny: 'Okay. How to fill the gap then. Any other thoughts, Melvin?'

*She summarizes and notes this so she can take it into the next step. Checks for more problems.*

Melvin: 'No, I'm happy enough doing a course. But is there any role-playing? I don't fancy making a fool of myself in front of a bunch of people I don't know.'

Jenny: 'Yes, there will be some. But it's not you that's on trial, it's the course. And you'll learn a lot from watching the others. The tutor I had handled it very well.'

*Honest reassurance.*

Melvin: 'Still . . . do they report back on us?'

Jenny: 'No, they don't. In fact, you'll be reporting back yourself, with your own action plan. And before you go off we'll have a meeting to work out what you really want to get out of it. We need to diarize that.'

*More detail that could have come into Step 2 but she has only just thought of it.*

Melvin: 'Right then.'

| 5. | Ask for his suggestions for |
|---|---|
| | (a) overcoming the problems |

Jenny: 'Now, filling the hole while you're away. Any suggestions Melvin?'

*A coaching question to get Melvin into a problem-solving frame of mind.*

Melvin: 'Well, if there's a big emergency they can always come to you. They'll deal with the little ones themselves.'

*He is on his mettle and so thinks of solutions.*

Jenny: 'Right, and the regular stuff?'

*Another coaching question.*

Melvin: 'It'll just have to wait, I suppose, there'll only be three days' worth.'

Continued on next page

Jenny: 'True, but can you see an opportunity in this – for developing your people?'

*Another coaching question. She sees the opportunity and wants him to grasp it.*

Melvin: 'What are you thinking of?'

Jenny: 'Well you can come back to a pile of paper and wade through it all, or you can come back to a pile of documents with their recommendations pinned on. Which would you prefer?'

*She makes this suggestion for his comments.*

*It's a leading question but reasonable in this context.*

Melvin: What, get them to look at my work, you mean?'

*Melvin picks up the idea,*

Jenny: 'Yes. You'll probably be able to agree with most of what they suggest, and that'll save you a lot of time and brain work.'

*Jenny expands on it,*

Melvin: 'Yes. Good idea. They can just take stuff in rotation, as it comes in.'

*and Melvin runs with it.*

> and (b) implementing the change,
>
> using a joint problem-solving approach.

Jenny: 'I think that's about it then Melvin. What's the next step, do you think?'

*Still coaching and letting Melvin take control with the main objectives accomplished.*

Melvin: 'Well, I'll read this lot but what about this meeting, the pre-course thing?'

Jenny: 'Set a date, you mean? Okay.'

Melvin: 'I'll just get my diary, Jenny, and I'll be right back.'

*This is the immediate follow-up. The meeting date will be the next.*

Jenny: 'Fine, come in when you're ready.'

See the next page for a check on the framework for Practical Leadership Skills.

That discussion about a training course took three minutes and forty seconds - without the comments. Check it against the framework for:

## PRACTICAL LEADERSHIP SKILLS.

See if you agree that the boss applied all seven of the all-the-time skills.

---

1. **Maintain or enhance the self-esteem of the employee.**

   Jenny talked about self-development, and showed she herself had needed the same training, as others did too.

2. **Don't attack the person,**
   **FOCUS ON THE PROBLEM.**

   There was no attacking. The problems had already been discussed in the performance review. Melvin solved his own problems with Jenny's coaching.

3. **Don't assume that the employee has committed an offence.**

   Jenny made no assumptions.

4. **Encourage the employee to express his opinions and make suggestions.**

   Opinions came out in Step 4 and suggestions in 5(a) and 5(b).
   Jenny deliberately kept these steps separated.

5. **Allow the employee adequate time to think through the problem and to suggest a solution.**

   Less than four minutes but Melvin solved the problem on emergencies. Jenny raised the idea (not new to her) for developing Melvin's staff and he took it up.

6. **Ensure that the employee has an appropriate action programme.**

   Jenny wanted Melvin to use the opportunity to develop his staff – as well as going on the course.

7. **Always set a specific follow-up date.**

   This is for when Melvin returns, at which time they will agree the date for the pre-course meeting and, very possibly, the date for the follow-up meeting.

---

# Notes

# 3. UNWELCOME WORK

The scene is a sloping building site where the Site Manager, Jack, has to talk with Bob, the leader of a small gang of bricklayers who are working at one end of the site. It is Friday morning and Jack approaches Bob where he is working on face brickwork on a long boundary wall. (Face brickwork is the good looking brickwork, the visible outer skin of a building or wall, that is tidily finished off.)

Both men know that this part of the work is ahead of schedule because they were able to start on it earlier than expected. This was due to a delay in the delivery of heavy building blocks for use on a retaining wall at the other end of the site.

> (Consider objective, implications, alternatives and discretion.)

Jack's overall objective is to ensure that the different parts of the building programme fit together as well as possible because completing parts out of sequence can cost time and money, and cause problems for the different trades.

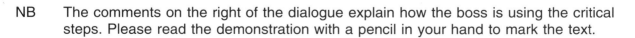

His objective for the discussion is to get under way a change from pleasant, satisfying work to less pleasant work.

One implication is that there may be some reluctance on the part of Bob and/or his bricklayers.

One alternative is to leave things as they are but that would conflict with the overall objective.

Jack has a fair amount of discretion as site manager. He could possibly delay this change for a day or two but he would still have to make it then.

NB   The comments on the right of the dialogue explain how the boss is using the critical steps. Please read the demonstration with a pencil in your hand to mark the text.

For a better understanding of the critical steps read the section, 'The Critical Steps Explained Further'.

| DIALOGUE | COMMENTS |
|---|---|
| **1.** **Explain the conditions which have brought about the need for change.** | |
| Jack: 'Morning Bob, give me a minute will you?' | *A friendly start.* |
| Bob: 'Right, okay.' | |
| Jack: 'You know those concrete blocks we've been waiting for, for the retaining wall at the other end?' | *This is part of the conditions.* |
| Bob: 'Oh, yes.' | |
| Jack: 'We'll be getting a load this afternoon.' | |
| Bob: 'About time as well.' | |
| Jack: 'Yes, we've been held up long enough. Anyway, we can start getting back on programme from Monday, Bob.' | *Another part of the conditions.* |
| Bob: 'Oh yes?' | |
| Jack: 'Well, there's about five thousand to lay, and if we can do that lot in, what, two weeks, we'll be back on programme and properly organized.' | *This is the need for change.* |
| Bob: 'Hmmmmmmmm.' | |
| **2.** **Explain the detail of the change and how it will affect the employee.** | |
| Jack: 'Now, I reckon that if you and all your lads start first thing Monday, we can crack it in the next fortnight. So you'll need to get to a tidy finish here today Bob.' | *This is the detail of the change and* *this is how Bob is affected.* |
| Bob: 'Hmm.' | |
| **3.** **If applicable, include a practical demonstration or teach the employee how to carry out the new process.** | *Bob does not need a demonstration of how to do heavy blocks or how to get to a tidy finish.* |

✓

| 4. | Ask the employee how he feels about the proposals: identify his major hang-ups and recognize any new problems. |
|---|---|

Jack: 'Can you see any problems with that?'

Bob: 'No, not really, but why do we have to put everybody up there, can't we keep both ends going?'

Jack: 'Do you think you've got enough men to do that *and* get back on programme – in two weeks?'

Bob: 'Well, not really, I suppose. But if we did I could keep George at this end – on the facing work.'

Jack: 'Why, what's with George?'

Bob: 'Well, you know what he's like. Some of this facing work's pretty fancy and George likes to think of himself as a bit of a master bricklayer. I don't think he's going to take too kindly to laying blocks.'

Jack: 'Well, I can understand that, could be awkward. Can you see any other problems Bob?'

Bob: 'Not really but, you know, we're on programme at this end, and if we put everybody down there, we could slip behind up here as well.'

Jack: 'Well, I think we're far enough in front here, Bob, for that not to be a problem. And that retaining wall really is critical.'

Bob: 'Well, I know that. But I don't see how we're going to get George down there. And even if we do I can't see him really pulling his weight.'

Jack: 'Right. Is it just that he prefers to do facings, or is there more to it than that?'

Bob: 'Well, he's getting on a bit now, and those blocks . . . they're high density, a bit on the heavy side, especially if we're having to push the work a bit.'

*Jack could just say, 'Okay' and walk off but, instead, checks for problems with this step.*

*A coaching question that gets Bob to think it through.*

*Probing.*

*Empathizing. Checking if there is anything else before moving into Step 5.*

*Jack has to stick with his own judgement here, and with his own position.*

*Bob really doesn't want to risk upsetting George.*

*Probing again.*

Jack: 'Well, I can see the position you're in with George.'

Empathizing again but . . .

---

5. Ask for his suggestions for

(a) overcoming the problems

---

Jack: 'But we've got to get back on programme. So, if George is the problem how can you turn him round? He's not going to like it either way.'

*Moves into 5(a) with gentle insistence based on Step 1. Asks for suggestions on George, a coaching question.*

Bob: 'Well . . . How about if you had a word with him?'

*A trap for Jack.*

Jack: 'Bob, ah, I think it's better if you do that.'

*Jack is not going to start doing Bob's work for him.*

Bob: 'Hmm, I suppose you're right. Well, all I can do is tell him what you've told me.'

*Faced with having to do it, Bob comes up with a solution.*

Jack: 'Yes, we need to get things in the right sequence.'

*Reinforcing the need for change.*

Bob: 'I could say that I wouldn't ask him if I didn't have to . . .'

Jack: 'But unless he does go up there?'

*Supporting Bob.*

Bob: 'We're not going to get back on programme.'

Jack: 'That's right. And he'll know that the other guys won't be too happy if they have to do all the heavy work.'

*Agreeing, with a reminder about teamwork.*

Bob: 'That's true enough.'

Jack: 'Still, what happens if he does get awkward?'

*Taking the possible problem a step further – contingency planning with a coaching question.*

Bob: 'Well, I don't know really.'

Jack: 'Well, what you can tell everybody, is that if we look like we're doing really well up there, then I'm happy for somebody to get back here again.'

*Joint problem-solving, a way of helping George to give in gracefully.*

Bob: 'And I can tell George it will be him?'

*That is Bob's decision.*

Jack: 'If he's done his share, why not?'

Bob: 'Yes, that'll keep him going.'

✓

| and | (b) implementing the change, |
| --- | --- |
| | using a joint problem-solving approach. |

Jack:   'So when do you reckon you can sort it out then?'

*Still coaching. Step 5(b) is about making it happen AND about creating a choice for the employee so far as possible.*

Bob:   'Well, give me a minute or two, let me think how I'm going to do it.'

Jack:   'That's okay. Just get George to give it a go. You'll handle it okay.'

*Building his self-esteem.*

Bob:   'Yes, all right then.'

Jack:   'Okay, and I'll be round again in a couple of hours, see how things are. Okay?'

*This follow-up date allows Jack to ensure that all is going well with the change. Or to take further action if it is not.*

Bob:   'Yes. See you later.'

See the next page for a check against the framework for Practical Leadership Skills.

That discussion took about three and a half minutes. Check it against the framework for:

**PRACTICAL LEADERSHIP SKILLS.**

See if you agree that the boss applied all seven of the all-the-time skills.

---

1.   **Maintain or enhance the self-esteem of the employee.**

   Jack helped Bob to think through to an action plan and showed confidence in him. The quick follow-up means that talking with George will not worry Bob for long.

2.   **Don't attack the person,**
     **FOCUS ON THE PROBLEM.**

   There was no attacking, not even of George. Jack first raised the problem of getting organized again, then dealt with Bob's problem.

3.   **Don't assume that the employee has committed an offence.**

   There were no assumptions about Bob's reluctance to tackle George. This keeps the conversation objective and on track.

4.   **Encourage the employee to express his opinions and make suggestions.**

   This is the deliberate use of Step 4 and Step 5 of the change framework.

5.   **Allow the employee adequate time to think through the problem and to suggest a solution.**

   A discussion shorter than three and a half minutes might not have got through to an appropriate action programme, simple though it is.

6.   **Ensure that the employee has an appropriate action programme.**

   Yes, and there is a contingency plan for George.

7.   **Always set a specific follow-up date.**

   In two hours because Jack needs early reassurance that the change is underway.

---

# 4. IMPROVING PERSONAL EFFECTIVENESS

Keith is an Area Manager who spends much of his time visiting retail units. He spends little time in his office where he shares a secretary with three other area managers who also are out a lot. Here he is talking with his secretary, Sarah during a visit to the office.

> (Consider objective, implications, alternatives and discretion.)

Keith's overall objective is to get more done with his time and to get better use from Sarah's time.

His objective for the discussion is to get things moving in the right direction and also to get Sarah really involved so that she will eventually become committed.

One implication is that Sarah will not want to lose an important skill.

He is open to alternatives which meet his objectives, and also wants Sarah to be able to choose from alternatives.

He has quite a lot of discretion about how he responds to the need for change. He also thinks that if he does not improve his effectiveness he may be unable to continue in the job, it will get on top of him and he could fail.

NB     The comments on the right of the dialogue explain how the boss is using the critical steps. Please read the demonstration with a pencil in your hand to mark the text.

For a better understanding of the critical steps read the section, 'The Critical Steps Explained Further'.

| DIALOGUE | COMMENT |
|---|---|
| **1.** Explain the conditions which have brought about the need for change. | |
| Keith: 'Sarah, I'm going to ask if you'll help me with something. Let me tell you what it's about, I'll tell you what I want you to do and then I'll ask how you feel about it, okay?' | *First asks for her help. Then indicates how he will go about it, showing she will be asked for her views. He 'sets out his stall'.* |
| Sarah: 'Okay.' | |
| Keith: 'It seems that I'm spending more and more time on the road, and less and less in the office. It's partly the traffic and partly due to having more units to manage.' | *Part of the conditions which have brought about the need for change.* |
| Sarah: 'Yes.' | |
| Keith: 'So a problem that we've both had is now getting worse; on the one hand me getting time with you for dictation, and, on the other hand, you being able to type stuff before I'm off out again.' | *A further part of the conditions. Sarah should be familiar with both.* |
| Sarah: 'Yes, and the others wanting their work at the same time.' | |
| Keith: 'That's right, it's bedlam when there's more than one of us in.' | *Keith empathizes and his agreement reinforces a further condition which has brought about a need for change.* |
| Sarah: 'Hmm.' | |
| Keith: 'Anyway, I thought we could make better use of time for both of us if I got myself an electronic memo, one of those little dictaphone machines. That way I could do a lot of dictation in the car, and even dictate notes when I'm in the units.' | *This leads into the detail of the change for Sarah.* |
| Sarah: 'I see.' | |
| **2.** Explain the detail of the change and how it will affect the employee. | |
| Keith: 'What it means for you Sarah, is that I'm asking you to learn a new skill, audio typing, but I would help you with that. The other thing is that you wouldn't be losing time when I'm dictating, and wondering what to say.' | *He switches now from the broad picture to the specific change and how it affects Sarah.*<br>*Offers help with the new skill, and a plus point.* |

Sarah: 'Oh, it's not that bad.'

Keith: 'Bad enough sometimes. And if I gave you one or two tapes when I come in we'd both have more freedom because we wouldn't have to get together for dictation time.'

*He sticks to the conditions and*
*offers another plus point.*

Sarah: 'Hmmm.'

Keith: 'Now, besides learning a new skill, Sarah, I'm going to ask if you will buy the equipment that you have to use.'

*Another way in which she is affected.*

Sarah: 'I don't know anything about it.'

| 3. | If applicable, include a practical demonstration or teach the employee how to carry out the new process. |
|---|---|

Keith: 'Well, Purchasing have got these three leaflets that are within budget, and they'll explain each type of system.'

*Keith hands these over. The text and pictures will explain the systems and alternatives far better than he will.*

Sarah: 'Thanks.'

Keith: 'What I thought was that, if you had a look at the office side of the equipment, you could ask what training there is at the same time. The whole range is available at Toothills.'

*When he says, 'What I thought' Keith is showing he is open to other thoughts.*
*Raises the question of training.*

Sarah: 'Toothills?'

Keith: 'Yes, just off Broadway. Now, what I've done, is tested all three of the *portable* dictating machines, and I'm okay with any of them.'

Sarah: 'Well, that's useful.'

| 4. | Ask the employee how he feels about the proposals; identify his major hang-ups and recognize any new problems. |
|---|---|

Keith: 'Yes, it means you can choose the sytem that suits you best. What do you think about it?'

*He has said all he wants to and now starts to work, very deliberately, at listening.*

---

Sarah: 'Well, I'm very happy doing shorthand. If we didn't have dictation then I wouldn't see much of you and the others at all.'

Keith: 'Yes, but it's all a bit pressured now isn't it? The time we get in future should be better quality time, when we can discuss things properly, Sarah.'

*He registers that time together is important to Sarah.*

Sarah: 'Am I making mistakes with my shorthand, is that it?'

Keith: 'No way. It's always been immaculate, no problems at all. It's simply saving time for both of us.'

*That was a real concern of Sarah's. She needs, and gets, reassurance.*

Sarah: 'What about training for you Keith?'

Keith: 'What do you mean?'

*Surprised, but probes.*

Sarah: 'Well, a friend of mine, her boss went over to a portable dictaphone. She couldn't hear what he said in the car and then, when she'd done the typing he came in at the end of the tape and said could she do another copy for somebody else.'

Keith: 'Ah, yes.'

*He has heard about this sort of thing.*

Sarah: 'So she had to go off to the copying machine. These days though it's all on the word processor so that's not a problem.'

Keith: 'Right. Cars are a bit quieter these days as well. And I'll make sure the window's closed, and I don't have the radio on.'

Sarah: 'Am I going to lose my shorthand?'

Keith: 'Well, there's three other managers, Sarah, who'll still be dictating.'

Sarah: 'Yes, but they'll see this with you and they'll all be wanting one.'

Keith: 'I wouldn't be surprised. That's your main concern is it, keeping up your shorthand?'

*He appreciates she likes using shorthand and doesn't want to lose the skill. This is not a work problem for her but could be a major personal hang-up.*

Sarah: 'Yes, I suppose so.'

Continued on the next page

| 5. | Ask for his suggestions for |
|---|---|
| | (a) overcoming the problems |

Keith: 'Okay. Even if we all went over to electronic memos, what ways can you see of using your shorthand?'

*Puts the problem back to Sarah with a coaching question. She is in a better position to come up with ideas and Keith doesn't have any.*

Sarah: 'Not a lot really. There's quick notes about mail, I suppose.'

Keith: 'And telephone messages.'

*Building on Sarah's thoughts.*

Sarah: 'Yes, and I make notes of instructions, and messages you all want me to pass to each other.'

*Good ideas breed more ideas*

*and*

Keith: 'And messages on the answering machine. There's still a fair bit to go at.'

*this is joint problem-solving.*

Sarah: 'Yes, but I'll lose my speed though.'

Keith: 'How fast will you need to be, if we're all using machines?'

*He puts things into perspective with another coaching question.*

Sarah: 'Yes, I see what you mean.'

Keith: 'And there'll always be emergencies when we have to dictate something over the telephone.'

*From no ideas at the start of this step, there are now several.*

Sarah: 'Yes, I suppose so.'

| and | (b) implementing the change, |
|---|---|
| | using a joint problem-solving approach. |

Keith: 'And you'll have a new skill. Sarah, I'd like to get into this just as quickly as possible. What's the next step do you think?'

*That problem now being dealt with, Keith can move forward with the plus of the new skill and choice for Sarah.*

Sarah: 'Well, I'd better have a look at these brochures, and then I'll get off to Toothills.'

Keith: 'Fine. Is there anyone here who can help, do you think?'

*A nice coaching question that gets Sarah to think.*

Sarah: 'Yes, now that you mention it. Doreen's boss uses a machine, I'll have a word with her.'

Keith: 'And for actually buying the gear, for both of us?'

Sarah: 'Well, if the budget's okay all we have to do is write 'portable and office dictaphone equipment' on the order form and I'll do the rest at Toothills.'

Keith: 'That's all right, then. Then there's training and tapes. How many tapes do we need?'

*By using questions Keith is getting action without having to give instructions.*

Sarah: 'Well, let me check on those things, and some spare batteries for you?'

Keith: 'Fine, sounds okay to me. When do you reckon I can pick it up then?'

*Looking for a plan with a timescale.*

Sarah: 'I should have it by, what, Wednesday. Who do I see in Purchasing?'

Keith: 'Samantha Renard knows all about it.'

Sarah: 'Okay then.'

Keith: 'Smashing. Okay, I'll be in on Thursday for sure. And you can tell me about the training then; and if you have any problems at all you can let me know.'

*Follow-up date is set – for the equipment and further discussion on training.*

Sarah: 'Okay. Are you ready for some old-fashioned dictation now?'

See the next page for a check against the framework for Practical Leadership Skills.

That discussion about effectiveness took about five minutes, not long for a change that will affect the secretary quite significantly. Check it against the framework for:

**PRACTICAL LEADERSHIP SKILLS**.

See if you agree that the boss applied all seven of the all-the-time skills.

1. **Maintain or enhance the self-esteem of the employee.**

   A good explanation plus assurances regarding no mistakes in her present work.

2. **Don't attack the person,**
   **FOCUS ON THE PROBLEM.**

   No attacking at all. Keith acknowledged Sarah's main concern and dealt with it. And he has achieved his objectives.

3. **Don't assume that the employee has committed an offence.**

   There were no assumptions from Keith.

4. **Encourage the employee to express his opinions and make suggestions.**

   This was okay with action steps coming from Sarah.

5. **Allow the employee adequate time to think through the problem and to suggest a solution.**

   Sarah thought through her own problem which fell away. She will see to the rest of the action.

6. **Ensure that the employee has an appropriate action programme.**

   Yes. Sarah can choose the equipment and will pursue the training.

7. **Always set a specific follow-up date.**

   This is Thursday when Keith will receive his equipment and hear about training.

## Notes

# 5. REDUCING OVERTIME

In this situation a maintenance manager, Edgar, is faced with tightening budget constraints and has to find cost savings within his operation. He has two shift managers, Andy and Brian, and each of them has several staff. He is now talking to them together.

(Consider objective, implications, alternatives and discretion.)

Edgar's overall objective is to cut costs. In this discussion, which is one of the agenda items for a weekly meeting, he wants to have an action plan agreed that will move him towards that overall objective.

The implications he has considered will show up in Steps 1 and 2.

He is open to alternative ways of cutting costs but as *additional ways*. His own idea is too strong to be set aside.

He has discretion as to whether he makes cuts gradually or quickly and deeply.

NB   The comments on the right of the dialogue explain how the boss is using the critical steps. Please read the demonstration with a pencil in your hand to mark the text.

For a better understanding of the critical steps read the section, 'The Critical Steps Explained Further'.

---

| DIALOGUE | COMMENTS |
|---|---|
| **1.** Explain the conditions which have brought about the need for change. | |

Edgar: 'We're on to costs now, gentlemen, and, quite simply I need your help in cutting them.'

*Switching to a new topic in the meeting, and asking for help in a non-threatening way.*

Brian: 'Haven't we saved ten per cent already, Edgar?'

Edgar: 'Yes, we have, and the squeeze is on to save another ten. The problem is that our product is going out the gate at a pound a case more than our main competitors so we risk losing business.'

*A clear and strong condition requiring change.*

Andy: 'Ah, we've heard that before.'

Edgar: 'True, but cost control is a constant part of the job. Everybody else is looking to cut costs as well, and Purchasing are looking at raw materials. We have to do our bit.'

*Showing they are not alone in making this change.*
*Showing firmness; it has to happen.*

Andy: 'Well, with us it seems that it's always our guys that suffer.'

Edgar: 'Okay, look. I'm open to ideas, but right now I want you to work on one thing, for a start.'

*Showing an open mind and firmness at the same time.*

Brian: 'What's that?'

Edgar: 'Well, three months ago we reduced your teams from ten to eight and one of your concerns was that you should be able to cover any problems with overtime. And I agreed.'

Andy: 'And we've been using it.'

Edgar: 'Right. But what I've noticed is that technicians have been putting themselves up for the overtime slots, four hours a shift for ten shifts a week, and they do it in advance.'

*Firm information. Another condition which has brought about the need for this change*

Brian: 'Well, we can't wait until it's too late.'

Edgar: 'If you think back Brian, the reason for booking in advance was to cover us for the drop from ten techs to eight. But if we book overtime in advance then people want their share. Just look at this for next week. They put the hours in all right but I'm not sure that they're putting much into the hours.'

*He shows the current overtime booking sheet. Step 3 is being overlaid on Step 1 here.*

Brian: 'How can you say that?'

Edgar: 'What I'm saying is that I'm not sure, but I *suspect* that we're in danger of entrenching another bad habit. We're booking overtime in advance when we have no way of knowing that we'll need it.'

*No accusation, but he is able to voice a suspicion.*

*This is difficult to argue with.*

Andy: 'You're not going to tell us to just cut it out are you?'

Edgar: 'No. But I want no unnecessary overtime at all. Right now we're paying premium rates on forty hours every week.'

*Quite firm.*

---

| 2. | Explain the detail of the change and how it will affect the employee. |
|---|---|

Edgar: 'What I do want you to do is cut out automatic overtime booking altogether and, instead, have a roster showing when people can expect to be *called on* for overtime. In other words it's like having people on call, but I'm saying that if a rostered technician is needed to do overtime then he would have known in advance that he *might* have to stay on.'

*Answering their question, 'What do you want from us?'*

Brian: 'A roster?'

Edgar: 'Yes. It doesn't mean that you can't *schedule* overtime work in advance where you know it has to happen. But there can be no asking people to fill an overtime slot when we don't know it will be needed.'

*Giving what they MAY do.*

Andy: 'So, if we decide on Monday that a machine has to be taken off-line on Wednesday for out-of-hours maintenance we can schedule the overtime it will need?'

---

✓

Edgar: 'If you have to, yes, but the guy doing it will be the one on the roster for the end of that shift.'

*Using the question to give more detail.*

Andy: 'Okay, I can see that.'

Edgar: 'I know this won't be popular with some folks. I know some do most of the overtime and some don't want to do any. And I know it puts more responsibility on you two. But a tight operation is safer than a slack one.'

*Showing negative implications*

*and a positive implication.*

Andy: 'But we don't want to get too tight.'

Edgar: 'Well, Andy, that will be up to you and Brian. You need to get as much work into normal hours as you can *before* you authorize overtime. Now, we'll have to formalize the change in contracts of employment, and we need to work out some form of compensation, but . .'

*More detail.*

| 3. | If applicable, include a practical demonstration or teach the employee how to carry out the new process. |
|---|---|

*Using next week's overtime booking sheet was a practical demonstration of the present situation.*

*Edgar believes the two shift managers need no demonstration of rosters.*

| 4. | Ask the employee how he feels about the proposals: identify his major hang-ups and recognize any new problems. |
|---|---|

Edgar: 'I want to ask how you feel about the idea?'

Brian: 'Who's going to tell the technicians about this?'

*Although Edgar has been firm he still needs to hear their thoughts.*

Edgar: 'Not an easy task, I agree.'

*Empathizing.*

Andy: 'You can say that again. One of my guys is very happy not doing overtime and the other three average, oh, about six hours a week. That's useful money over a month.'

Brian: 'And I've got just the same situation.'

Edgar: 'Okay, we'll have to work on that one. Can you see any other problems?'

Brian: 'We'll have to know, *before* the roster man goes home, if anything needs to be done.'

Edgar: 'Yes, any difficulty there?'

Andy: 'I shouldn't think so, no.'

Brian: 'What about the overtime that's booked already? We can't renege on that.'

Edgar: 'I agree, if you've made the offer and people have accepted, that's that. But no more booking forms to go up.'

Andy: 'When does this come into operation?'

Edgar: 'We need to give four weeks' formal notice, but only after everybody's been told – and we want to go about that properly.'

Andy: 'So what about in between? There'll be two or three weeks without overtime booked but before we get on to the roster system.'

Edgar: 'Yes, we need to sort that out. Do you have any other thoughts?'

Brian: 'Well, cutting a lot of overtime is like losing one technician, isn't it? How about that?'

Edgar: 'What? Lose one and still share overtime among the rest, is that what you mean?'

Brian: 'We'd get the work done.'

Edgar: 'Brian, we'd still have *uncontrolled* overtime and we'd still have to cut it later. We've got to tackle it now.'

Brian: 'Yes, okay.'

Edgar: 'Andy?'

Andy: 'No, it's just going to be difficult, that's all.'

Edgar: 'Okay, you've highlighted two problems. One is telling the guys and the other is how to handle the gap between the present system and the new one. And then there's compensation for standing by.'

---

*Not arguing. Wanting to get all the problems before starting on solutions.*

*Brian was just thinking aloud.*

*Edgar voices his agreement rather than letting Brian wonder where he (Edgar) stands.*

*Edgar could have mentioned this in Step 2 but didn't think of it. But this step, 4, is a safety net for such things.*

*Makes a further note of a problem to be solved. Checks for others.*

*Checks his understanding.*

*Sticks to his position.*

*Edgar ensures Andy has a chance to raise his thoughts.*

*Summarizing to give a new platform for moving forward.*

*Edgar has realized this last one himself.*

---

5.    Ask for his suggestions for

(a) overcoming the problems

Edgar:  ' Let's take the gap first. How can we handle that?'

Brian:  'We still need overtime to be able to get essentials done.'

Edgar:  'I agree, but only after you've made sure that they can't be done during the shift.'

Andy:  'Yes, okay. Let's assume that we'd still need two hours per shift, maximum.'

Brian:  'After we let the four hour slots fall away?'

Andy:  'Yes. We could ask for volunteers for those two hour slots, and that would give us a transition period.'

Edgar:  'For the period of notice?'

Andy:  'Yes, and by then Brian and I would have more positive control.'

Edgar:  'And during the transition you'll have reduced the need for overtime anyway?'

Andy:  'Yes, that's right.'

Brian:  'In fact, we ought to start doing that straightaway.'

Edgar:  'Yes, you're right. And that will show what savings can be made, won't it?'

Brian:  'I suppose it will, at least we can get a measure on it.'

Andy:  'You know, I think we should make a public target, for the whole department, of as little overtime as possible, and get everybody committed to bringing it down, and holding it down.'

Edgar:  'Yes, that would be a good measure of success in doing the main job. Okay. we can make that part of the discussion. How do we stand so far Brian?'

*Moves from problem-finding (albeit amicable) to problem-solving with a coaching question.*

*Agreeing on essentials, denying inessentials.*

*Two team members working together.*

*Seeking clarification.*

*Putting thoughts into their minds with a suggestion put as a coaching question.*
  *Accepting the idea.*

*And reinforcing it.*

*Highlighting the benefit.*

*Asking for a summary to check understanding.*

| | | |
|---|---|---|
| Brian: | 'I think we both have overtime booked in four hour slots until the end of next week?' | *Checks with his colleague.* |
| Andy: | 'Right.' | |
| Brian: | 'So we announce that for the next, what, three weeks, we'll be offering two hour slots and then, from the 16th, we'll be on a roster of people standing by for overtime.' | *Sums up the combined proposal.* |
| Edgar: | 'Andy?' | |
| Andy: | 'Yes, that's how I see it. Could we say that people can still swap on the roster?' | *Adds another idea.* |
| Edgar: | 'I don't see why not, as long as we always roster everyone because, during holidays, people might not be able to swap.' | *Agrees – with a proviso.* |
| Brian: | 'I think Andy and I both need to handle this at the same time, at shift changeover.' | |
| Edgar: | 'Tomorrow?' | |
| Andy: | 'Provided we have something to say on how we're going to compensate them for being on call.' | *The remaining problem.* |
| Edgar: | 'Okay. Any ideas on that one? There's no doubt in my mind that people should be compensated if they can't say they'll be home on time.' | *Asks a coaching question to put the thinking back to his team members, but gives them a starting point.* |
| Brian: | 'If they do work over I think they should get a minimum of two hours at premium rates, even if they only do fifteen minutes.' | |
| Andy: | 'And in units of fifteen minutes beyond two hours.' | |
| Edgar: | 'Okay, we certainly don't want a four hour minimum or that defeats the whole object. What about a rostering payment?' | *Edgar can assess their ideas as he listens. By coaching them he does not have to come up with his own ideas, and therefore does not lose objectivity by fighting for them.* |
| Brian: | 'Well, a friend of mine is in a computer department and he gets rostered on to standby, and he gets a quarter of the overtime rate for every hour on standby.' | |
| Edgar: | 'So we need to check what happens here. But, really, this is *not* a standby situation because if the rostered technician isn't needed they've finished for the day. And if they are needed they'll get paid for at least two hours.' | *Clarifies the situation.* |

Brian: 'Yes, but they can't plan on an evening out if they're on the roster.'

Edgar: 'Hmmm.'                    *Taking time to think.*

Brian: How about a round fiver a time for being    *And allowing more ideas to come*
rostered. We'd reckon to save on the hours    *up.*
worked, and we could probably cut total
overtime costs by fifty per cent, so it pays
for itself – easily.'

Andy: 'And the fiver is for being rostered, they
sort it out between themselves if they
swap.'

Edgar: 'Let's try that. A fiver is a small part of the    *Edgar goes along with the fiver but*
old payment. Okay, but we have to save    *sticks on his targeted saving.*
that fifty per cent, at least.'

Andy: 'We'll be able to go firm on that when we're
really controlling it but I can't see any
problem.'

---

| and | (b) implementing the change, |
| | using a joint problem-solving approach. |

---

Edgar: 'So, how do you reckon to put it to the guys    *Moving from discussion to action,*
then?'    *with another coaching question.*

Brian: 'I think we need to liaise about the timing.'

Edgar: 'Right. And just to make sure you're both
singing from the same hymn sheet and    *Getting Andy to sum up the points*
we're all agreed, for the shift changeover    *means Edgar can assess his*
tomorrow, can we have a written summary    *understanding.*
of the key points – Andy?'

Andy: 'Okay. I'll work up my notes and give you
both a copy. I've got background, overall
objective, detail, timing, gap, payments and
compensation for being rostered?'    *Here Edgar looks to Brian for*
    *confirmation or disagreement.*

Brian: 'Yes.'

Andy: 'Reactions, problems, ideas.'

Edgar: 'That's fine. And talking about ideas, can
you ask your teams to bend their minds to
this cost-cutting business? It's in all our
interests.'

---

Andy: 'Okay. That's in as well. I doubt we'll get much to start with but yes, we'll be having follow-up meetings.'

Edgar: 'Okay Brian?'

Brian: 'Well, I'll be surprised if we can't come up with something between us.'

Edgar: 'Okay. Andy, I'm going to suggest that you check your list of key points with Brian before you come to me and if you have any questions give me a ring.'

*This will save time for Edgar as they can sort out any disagreements before they see him.*

Andy: 'Okay.'

Edgar: 'By ten in the morning? Does that suit you?'

*This is for tomorrow.*

Andy: 'Yes, that gives the three of us time to communicate if we have to.'

Edgar: 'And I'll check if any other department has a similar situation. In the meantime, thanks very much to both of you. I know it will be hard work for a while but I'm happy you can handle it. What's next now?'

*Payroll Department will be able to help him on this one.*

*Moving to the next item on the agenda.*

See the next page for a check against the framework for Practical Leadership Skills.

That team discussion on reducing overtime took about eight minutes, quite long but much was achieved. Check it against the framework for:

**PRACTICAL LEADERSHIP SKILLS.**

See if you agree that the boss applied all seven of the all-the-time skills.

---

1. **Maintain or enhance the self-esteem of the employee.**

   A good explanation and involvement, plus good reinforcement at the end.

2. **Don't attack the person,**
   **FOCUS ON THE PROBLEM.**

   No attacking at all. There were four problems addressed in turn: reason for change, the gap between the old and the new, communicating, appropriate compensation.

3. **Don't assume that the employee has committed an offence.**

   Okay. Edgar suspects that the team is in danger of getting into a bad habit and has said so but has not turned suspicion into assumption..

4. **Encourage the employee to express his opinions and make suggestions.**

   Very careful listening to opinions by Edgar who then worked through each problem in turn to get their suggestions.

5. **Allow the employee adequate time to think through the problem and to suggest a solution.**

   Until ten o'clock tomorrow to raise any further problems and ideas. Eight minutes was plenty of time for initial ideas which will, no doubt, be refined.

6. **Ensure that the employee has an appropriate action programme.**

   They will agree their approach, put it in writing, and also look for more ideas.

7. **Always set a specific follow-up date.**

   No later than 10 a.m. tomorrow. At that time they will probably agree a new follow-up date to report back.

---

# 6. A NEW WAY OF TENDERING

In a medium sized construction company Ralph, the Managing Director, wants to introduce a fundamental change and is talking with the Department Head who has most influence with the other department heads. This is David.

---

(Consider objective, implications, alternatives and discretion.)

---

The overall objective is to get more business at less cost as tendering uses considerable resources.

The objective of the discussion is to test out an idea with David so as to be able to make an effective presentation to all the department heads. This will also have the effect of getting David on his side if there should be much opposition from the other people.

The implications are what he wants to find out from David.

He is open to alternative ways of achieving the overall objective and is ready to see his own idea amended.

Ralph has total discretion in what is done but he really has to get the business more focused.

NB    The comments on the right of the dialogue explain how the boss is using the critical steps. Please read the demonstration with a pencil in your hand to mark the text.

For a better understanding of the critical steps read the section, 'The Critical Steps Explained Further'.

---

| DIALOGUE | COMMENTS |
|---|---|
| **1.** Explain the conditions which have brought about the need for change. | |

Ralph: 'David, I've got a couple of ideas about the way we bid for tenders and I'd like to get your views before I go any further with it.'

*Showing David that his opinion is valued and that Ralph's idea is not cast in stone.*

David: 'Fine, what do you have in mind?'

Ralph: 'Well, let me tell you why I think it's important, then I'll outline my ideas, and then I'll ask how you feel about it, okay?'

*Ralph 'sets out his stall' by indicating three parts to the discussion and, effectively, asking David to listen until invited to come in.*

David: 'Okay, then.'

Ralph: 'Well, you know how much work goes into tenders and all the chasing-up. And, as you also know, the success rate is something like one in seven, so six out of seven are a waste of money.'

David: 'That's the nature of the business, Ralph. '

Ralph: 'Well, at the moment we tender for everything we're capable of doing. What we're *not* doing is targeting those that we *really* want to get. And when we do get a job the people who run it have a big learning curve because they usually come to it cold.'

*Ralph avoids the mistake of attacking David whose thinking is not up with his own. Ralph presses ahead with his case.*

David: 'Well, how can they be involved before we have the job?'

Ralph: '*Getting* jobs is what I'm on about because, with competition as it is, we could easily get nothing out of a whole run of tenders. And when we do get a job it's quite likely to be more trouble than it's worth. And that could put us out of business. We *have* to improve our chances of getting *better* jobs.'

*Ralph develops his theme in response to David.*

David: 'So what do you have in mind then?'

> 2. Explain the detail of the change and how it will affect the employee.

Ralph: 'Right, let me show what it would mean for you David, and the other department heads. How we go about tenders at the moment is like this. We have jobs A through G?'

David: 'Yes.'

Ralph: 'We have estimators working on each one.'

David: 'Okay.'

Ralph: 'Planning would have people putting time into each tender to some extent. And so on through Buying, Quantity Surveying and Line Management.'

David: 'Right, so what's your idea then?'

Ralph: 'Well, that's the method we use. And when you consider that all these people sit in their own departments, we also have a communication problem. I'm not saying they don't talk to each other, it's just harder.'

David: 'Hmm, mm.'

Ralph: 'Now, my idea is this. We have to consider, at *our* level, what jobs we really want to win; the clients, consultants, management problems and so on. Once we've done that we don't work on seven or eight tenders, but just on the two or three that we really want.'

David: 'Well, yes, makes sense.'

Ralph: 'Say we decide on these two. Before we start on the tender I want us to nominate *a team* that will work on it together. They can really focus on what the client wants, they can do better presentations, and they're off to a flying start if we do get the job.'

David: 'I see.'

Ralph: 'And the team should be seconded to the line manager who'll eventually run the contract, if we get it.'

*Ralph has finished with background information and now switches to the detail. He sketches what he is saying on a piece of paper - below.*

A  B  C  D  E  F  G

EST.

PLAN

BUY

QS

LINE

*Ralph is overlaying Step 2 with Step 3 - '. . . include a practical demonstration. . .'*

 B  C  D  E  F

EST.

PLAN

BUY

QS

LINE

✓

David: 'So my staff would be responsible to line managers, is that what you mean?'

Ralph: 'For a specific project, yes, and sooner rather than later, so that the line manager has a more cohesive team from the start. If they get their heads together they can work out how we can do a better job for the client than the opposition.'

David: 'Well, I can see what you mean.'

Ralph: 'So what you have is a line manager, with the others coming into the team at different stages, and out again, as they do now. But all of them being consulted right from the start.'

David: 'What happens if, say, a buyer has to duck out sooner than expected?'

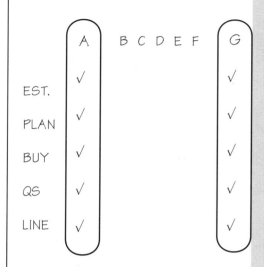

Ralph: 'Let me pick that up in a minute, David, because the last point is where they work. Right now people are split up in their own offices, working for their own department rather than the project.'

*Ralph, having added more to his sketch, notes the question but defers it so he can finish his explanation. David will then have a better basis for asking questions and contributing ideas later.*

David: 'Hmmmm.'

Ralph: 'What I'm suggesting is team members *not* being in their departments but in *team* areas. And, if we have the general offices made into open plan, these can change, as and when needed.'

David: 'That's a fair bit of work.'

Ralph: 'Well, there's two things, David. Focused, fluid teams working on fewer tenders and a combined, open plan office to facilitate communication and movement.'

*Ralph sums up the whole proposal.*

| 3. | If applicable, include a practical demonstration or teach the employee how to carry out the new process. |
|---|---|

*Ralph has already used a sketch of jobs and teams to illustrate his idea.*

✓

> 4.    Ask the employee how he feels about the proposals: identify his major hang-ups and recognize any new problems.

David:  'Hmmmm.'

Ralph:  'Anyway, I'd like to have your thoughts before I go any further, David. You raised the question of people having to leave a team early?'

*Ralph has finished presenting information and now switches to listening - and working at that. He shows he noted the earlier question.*

David:  'Yes, what I was thinking was, suppose someone in a team goes sick or something?'

Ralph:  'Okay, let me note that . . . that's drop outs.'

*Shows he is taking things seriously.*

David:  'And what if we find that someone has to be in two teams, they won't be able to do justice to both.'

Ralph:  'That's a nice thought. In two teams at once, okay.'

*Acknowledges an important point he had not considered himself.*

David:  'Really, though, Ralph, what are they going to do that they don't do now?'

Ralph:  'Quite a lot David. They'll be working as a team rather than alone on a task that has a six chances in seven of failing. They'll do the job better as a *project team* because they know they'll go through to finish it off if we get it. And, as a team, they'll identify some problems early so they can impress clients with the solutions. And that should help to get the job.'

*Ralph is now clarifying important motivational factors plus one result of teamworking. All make his proposal more worthwhile.*

David:  'Yes, good one. But have we got the people to make up teams when we want them?'

Ralph:  'Well, we'd be spending *less* time on tenders overall, so we'd have a better chance of making dedicated teams, with better quality time. But, yes, it won't be easy.'

*Another plus point that Ralph will use in later presentations.*

David:  'Well, I'm just thinking about trainees, Ralph, we might have nobody to put them with.'

Ralph: 'Yes, I see. Right, and that would apply to other departments as well, besides yours. Anything else you can think of David?'

*Makes a further note.*

*Checks before moving to the next step.*

David: 'Not just now, no.'

Ralph: 'Okay, let's see. You've mentioned drop-outs before the job's finished.'

*Reading from his notes.*

David: 'Yes.'

Ralph: 'Being in two teams at once?'

David: 'Yes.'

Ralph: 'And looking after the occasional trainee.'

David: 'Yes, and what about who owns the people on secondment.'

*The summarizing by Ralph prompts a further thought.*

Ralph: 'What are you thinking of there?'

*A probing question.*

David: 'Well, if a guy goes sick or has a pay query, who follows it up?'

Ralph: 'Right. That's four things then. Anything the other Heads might come up with?'

*Makes another note. Seeks to anticipate further problems*

David: 'Can't think of anything right now'

*Ralph can now move on. There are four work problems but no hang-ups of a personal nature.*

---

| 5. | Ask for his suggestions for |
|---|---|
| | (a) overcoming the problems |

---

Ralph: 'Okay, let's see who owns them first. How do you handle things when people are on site now?'

*States the problem and asks a question, a coaching question that will help to get to a solution.*

David: 'Yes, I keep in touch.'

Ralph: 'Telephone?'

David: 'And visits, on a regular basis.'

Ralph: 'Could you keep doing that?'

David: 'Don't see why not, so long as the line managers know what to expect.'

Ralph: 'Okay, I can make that clear. Then there's people dropping out, before they've done his bit. Bound to happen from time to time, I suppose. How do we crack that one David?'

David: 'Same as we do now, I expect. If a guy goes sick on site we have to get someone else in and bring him up to speed.'

Ralph: 'And who does that?'

David: 'Well, it's the site manager, plus me or a senior guy. One of us knows what's going on.'

Ralph: 'And the line managers should know what's happening, with just a small team.'

David: 'Yes, that's true. Will they have regular meetings, and minutes?'

*This question might have come up under Step 4 but it can be dealt with in Step 5.*

Ralph: 'I don't know about the minutes, but if we want real flexibility they'd better have frequent meetings, because we might have to take a guy off anyway.'

David: 'Good idea. And we can plan for leave cover and placements.'

Ralph: 'Of course we can. I'll make a note of that. Then I've got, what do we do if someone is in two teams at once? That could well happen.'

*Another point to cover in his presentation to the other department heads. Then to the third problem with another coaching question.*

David: 'Could you have one line manager leading two teams?'

Ralph: 'We certainly could.'

David: 'So, it works both ways. If one person is working for two different leaders they'll just have to negotiate, what do you think.?'

*Negotiating for resources is a fact of everyday working life.*

Ralph: 'I think you're right, David, I agree. Now, we're left with trainees. Nobody to put them with. But only now and again, I should think.'

*He makes his agreement explicit and, with the third problem dealt with, moves on to the fourth.*

David: 'Yes, we could have a trainee attached to Frank, say, and then Frank get's pulled away. One spare trainee to look after.'

---

Ralph: 'Might it be useful if the trainee went with him?'

David: 'Aaahmm. Yes. He'd be doing the same work, I suppose.'

Ralph: 'Better for the teamwork aspect, eh?'

David: 'True, no problem.'

*Joint problem-solving with a suggestion worded as a question. Ralph is keen to turn problems into opportunities.*

---

| and | (b) implementing the change, |
|---|---|
| | using a joint problem-solving approach. |

*What was thought likely to be a problem turns out to be no problem. Working it through is better than ignoring it or trying to belittle it.*

Ralph: 'How soon do you think we could move over to this new system then?'

David: 'Well, as soon as we've got the open plan office, and some good jobs lined up to tender for.'

*Another switch, with a coaching question, to move towards the next step.*

Ralph: 'Okay, anything else we need to get it going?'

David: Not that I can think of right now.'

*A good check question.*

Ralph: 'Okay. So we're looking at the end of the month probably.'

David: 'Don't see why not.'

Ralph: Right. What I'll be doing, is raising this at the next meeting, on Monday, and we'll take it from there. Will you think about it until then?'

David: 'Okay.'

*Another coaching question.*

Ralph: 'And if you think of anything could you get in touch before the meeting, by eight thirty?'

David: 'Yes, right.'

*This follow-up date is specifically for David, but only if he thinks of something.*

Ralph: You've been a really big help, David, thanks very much. See you Monday.'

See the next page for a check against the framework for Practical Leadership Skills

That discussion on a new way of tendering was quite complex and took about eight minutes. Check it against the framework for

# PRACTICAL LEADERSHIP SKILLS.

See if you agree that the boss applied all seven of the all-the-time skills.

---

**1.    Maintain or enhance the self-esteem of the employee.**

Self-esteem would have been enhanced by Ralph seeking David's advice.

**2.    Don't attack the person,**
        **FOCUS ON THE PROBLEM.**

No attacking at all. The basic problem was described in the need for change. Other problems were noted and handled in turn.

**3.    Don't assume that the employee has committed an offence.**

There were no bad assumptions from Ralph. In fact, he assumed that David would be able to contribute.

**4.    Encourage the employee to express his opinions and make suggestions.**

The whole framework for *Overcoming Resistance to Change* is designed to apply this critical skill and Ralph did so.

**5.    Allow the employee adequate time to think through the problem and to suggest a solution.**

Eight minutes of **focused** discussion was ample at this stage.

**6.    Ensure that the employee has an appropriate action programme.**

David will give it more thought until Monday.

**7.    Always set a specific follow-up date.**

That is 8.30 a.m. on Monday but only if David has more thoughts on the subject.

---

## Notes

# COMPARISONS WITH SITUATIONS AT YOUR WORKPLACE

You can use the demonstrations, which are summarized below, to make comparisons with your own situation at work. After those we'll look at a couple of other cases.

### 1. A problem with tax

This is a change that *has* to be made to comply with official requirements but it is still sensible to explain what the organization stands to gain or lose.

> Do you have to bring in any changes required by rules or regulations? How could you explain the benefits of following those rules or regulations?

### 2. Going on a training course

This is about making it easier for someone to accept a 'has to happen' change when there could be understand-able reluctance.

> Do you have any changes coming up where it would pay to look closely at the implications, and stress the plus points, eg the four star hotel? What are they?

### 3. Unwelcome work

This is about getting a junior manager to make a change where he anticipates difficulty; then coaching him when he asks for help in speaking to his own staff.

> How can you ensure that your junior managers (or yourself if you have no juniors) prepare properly for a change discussion where difficulties are anticipated?

### 4. Improving personal efficiency

This is about someone possibly losing, or at least reducing, a well established skill, and learning a new one – with the risks which that entails for the employee.

> You may have similar changes pending. What plus points can you offer with the changes that you will have to bring in?

## 5. Reducing overtime

Here a boss 'grasps the nettle' of really unwelcome change but works to get the help of his junior managers, and reduce the impact on the other people affected.

> Are there any situations where change is really urgent and you should be 'grasping the nettle'? If so, what are they? And how can you sensibly reduce the impact on the people affected?

## 6. A new way of tendering

This boss enlisted the aid of one of his people to test an idea *and* to improve his presentation to the whole group. This is sometimes called 'office politics'.

> What important changes do you have to make where it would be sensible to get someone on your side by first trying out the idea with them? What are the changes and who are the influential people?

## 7. Having it done to you

As a team member hearing a presentation or proposal for change you naturally have responsibility for seeking clarity by asking questions and, perhaps, by summarizing. This is especially true when a proposal has not been circulated before the meeting.

If you are not happy about some aspect of a proposal you may take one of two paths.

> You could simply express your concern about that part of the proposal, and wait for the proposer to note your concern before moving forward into Step 5 and asking for your ideas to overcome it. But is the proposer using this framework or something similar?

> Or (if that does not work) you may have to put forward a counter-proposal for that aspect of the change.

Either way, because someone has spent a lot of time – and ego – putting together the original proposal, you will need to put forward your own idea with care. Can you think of a better way than to use the framework for Overcoming Resistance to Change? Circle one.

YES          NO

The chances are, however, that you will be able to agree with 90% of the proposal so why not emphasize the areas of agreement in Step 1 *before* you focus on the proposal's problem in the same step? Step 2 is your own idea and the other steps follow on. Even though you may have had little preparation time you should still use Step 3 where you can.

---

Can you think of any occasions where you have been unhappy with someone else's proposal but have not been able to get your own idea organized or accepted? How would you handle such a situation in future?

---

> If you fail to challenge a potential problem at once you may never have another chance; by the time you organize yourself people will already have put time into the change and will be hard to shift to a new track – if it is possible at all.

# THE CRITICAL STEPS
# EXPLAINED FURTHER

If you attended a workshop you would be able to practise using the framework for Overcoming Resistance to Change, plus the framework of Practical Leadership Skills, and to observe others doing the same. You would also receive coaching (as needed) on handling changes that you personally want to bring about.

You would see how the frameworks can be used, very flexibly, in a range of different live situations of concern to participants. You would also see how much lies behind these critical steps and the Practical Leadership Skills.

Some of what you would learn in a workshop is explained, in the following pages, in the context of each critical step. The Coaching Questions which come later invite you to test the framework for yourself. Let us start with the thinking/planning stage.

---

**(Consider objective, implications, alternatives and discretion)**

---

This thinking/planning stage may take five seconds or less. With bigger changes it may take five weeks or more.

**OBJECTIVE** has two meanings:

- The objective of the change itself. What are you trying to achieve and why? How does it fit in with your department's main purpose?

- Your objective *for the discussion*. Do you want just an early reaction from the employee, or must they go away and think about the change, or make an action plan right now? Or do you want to make the first of several moves?

For both types of objective you need to ask if the objective can be achieved in one go, or does it need to be broken down into a series of mini-objectives?

*(Consider objective, implications, alternatives and discretion) (continued)*

What are the **IMPLICATIONS** of making the change?

- Some people may have to learn new skills or lose current ones, some may have vested interests to safeguard. How will you handle these things?

- A change in one place may impact on things and people in other places, for example a change in an incentive or reward scheme will affect the wages department for sure. But it may affect other departments with similar schemes. Can you check this out?

- Ask what can go wrong, so that you can make contingency plans.

- Ask if the change may contradict something else that is happening, eg making people redundant in one area whilst recruiting in another.

- What will you do if resistance is too great? Are you prepared for the hassle of pushing it through? Will you have support from the people who matter? How can you test that?

What **ALTERNATIVES** are there?

- Are there other ways of achieving what you want to achieve? Have you checked? Have you tried to generate alternatives? If you can't get what you want will you settle for less? Or for something different? Are you open to new ideas or (blindly) locked into your own?

What **DISCRETION** do you have?

- In implementing change from above, what freedom do you have to achieve results in your own way or at your own pace?

*(Consider objective, implications, alternatives and discretion) (continued)*

You can see that the time needed for this thinking and planning stage will depend on:

- The extent of the change, ie its depth and complexity, the number of people involved, etc.

- The time scale for the change, ie whether its implementation is some time ahead, or if it is to happen quickly; whether it will happen in stages, and so on.

If you can see the need for big change *before* it becomes pressing, you stand a better chance of introducing it smoothly.

The further you look into the future, the more vague the details will be. But this gives you more time to involve people in shaping the change to meet the conditions which have brought about the need for it.

How you use this critical step for planning will therefore depend on your own anticipation, and on the extent and time scale of the change. Better to think about it sooner rather than later.

We now move to the face-to-face steps used in the discussion itself.

## 1. Explain the conditions which have brought about the need for change.

Without the information in this step (which sometimes may be very brief) you cannot expect the employee to accept much responsibility for their part of the change, nor to fully commit to it.

Here you set the scene, show respect for the employee's need for involvement, indicate the importance of the change, and generally 'tune them in'. You give the reasons and/or the values behind the change. You show if this is something that *must* happen (a clear, powerful need for change) or something which you only think *should* happen. You show how firm or how flexible you are.

If you cannot do this step with conviction, you should not be initiating the change – or you have not fully understood change coming from above. You show here your enthusiasm for the change; or the lack of it.

Pause for a moment and give some thought to the future.

- Think about the way things are going now and where present trends will take you if they continue.

- Look at what you and your organization are doing now and ask what the competition is doing.

- Ask how customer needs may change.

- Ask what new technology will make possible for you.

- How do you and the organization need to change to meet the challenges which the future will bring?

At this point you don't need to have any answers, you simply need to recognize the conditions which are bringing about the need for change. HOW to change is something you need to think about, but recognizing the need for change is the starting point at which you can choose to bring in your team to also think about solutions.

Continued on next page

*1. Explain the conditions which have brought about the need for change. (continued)*

Anticipating change means that, to some extent, you can reduce future effects now. As one example: if you believe new technology will mean fewer, but more highly trained, people there are several things which your colleagues or staff may start to work on. In this example you may:

- research training methods to handle the new technology,

- control staff intake to those willing to be trained for new technology,

- look at options for displacing people who do not want to be retrained,

- consider space requirements for fewer people, etc.

---

**2. Explain the detail of the change and how it will affect the employee.**

---

After Step 1 sets the scene this step gets down to the nitty-gritty. You answer the employee's questions, 'What must I do?' and, 'How do I gain or lose?' You should anticipate other questions which the employee may raise and answer them here. Note that you should not be telling the employee *how* to do things, only *what* to do, otherwise you are doing their thinking for them. If necessary, any teaching comes in the next step.

If the change may bring any disadvantages for the employee you should be open about these and try to bring out any corresponding benefits.

If you are asking them to do difficult things this is where you assure them of your support and indicate your confidence in them.

It is also useful to say how people will NOT be affected. This shows what is remaining constant, reduces worries, and helps to focus on what *does* need to be done.

The employee may ask questions as you work through this step. This could distract you so acknowledge the questions, but say you will handle them later. Note them and bring them up again in Step 4.

---

> **3. If applicable, include a practical demonstration or teach the employee how to carry out the new process**.

Steps 1 and 2 are usually one-way. This can be hard work, requiring a lot of energy. But sometimes you may overlay one or both of those steps with this one; talking and demonstrating at the same time.

A picture is worth a thousand words so use anything at all that will aid understanding, eg sketches, drawings, flipcharts, pictures, models. These help the employee to understand and so make a meaningful contribution.

You can tell a person what training will be provided, take them to see a new process operating elsewhere, or do quick and easy training there and then. Or you may consider courses, open learning (video, audio, text, computer based), supplier training, etc.

If, with 'the new process', you are entering upon something new and risky then training and support show you have thought things through, and that you want the employee to succeed; you show your commitment to those taking risks.

In thinking about this step you may ask, about each individual involved in the change, 'Do they have the potential to do what we want them to do?' Most times the answer is 'Yes' but, if not, you have another implication of making the change.

This step leads you to look at the scale of the communication and training requirement. You may decide that managers should be better trained to handle the future. This may result in offering help for them to obtain a recognized qualification. You may also talk with some institute of learning to adapt one of their courses to suit your people.

Steps 1, 2 and 3 lead towards understanding but may not, on their own, gain agreement or support. For that you need real involvement and that comes in the next steps.

> **4.  Ask the employee how he feels about the proposals; identify his major hang-ups and recognize any new problems.**

This step is really, *really* important. It can also be very hard because, having thought through the change, you may resent anyone questioning your plans and ideas. But concerns raised now by employees mean potential problems can be handled before they arise, so welcome and explore these concerns.

Let us not exaggerate. With simple or routine changes the employee may say, 'No problem, leave it to me.' But beyond that the employee will generally have something to raise. However, if they surprise you by *not* raising questions this could be because they think they understand when they really don't. Or they could just be too polite. You then have to ask check questions yourself, eg 'How do you think the (whotsit) may be affected?'.

It's difficult to deal with vague problems voiced by employees so bring them into sharp focus. With a stream of concerns or questions, focus on them one by one. You will be able to easily give answers to some of them. Where you can't, you may be looking at a major hang-up (of a personal nature) or a new problem (connected with the work itself).

"Identify" means "to put a label on", or tag, which you can do by noting a key word to come back to later. Listen well, suspending your impatience to move forward, whilst taking the trouble to explore the employee's concerns - and empathize where appropriate. Resistance can be prolonged unless you show empathy for the employee's feelings.

"Recognize" means to acknowledge, appreciate, realize. You cannot know as much about a job as the person doing it, so recognize any work problems *without* rebuking yourself for not having thought of them. After all, this is a team effort; at this stage you are discussing a proposal and inviting comments.

"Identifying" and "recognizing" are facilitated by *summarizing* - see later.

*4. Ask the employee how he feels about the proposals;
identify his major hang-ups and recognize any new
problems. (continued)*

You can only anticipate, and cover in Steps 2 and 3, what
*you* think of. This step is a safety net for the things that
only the employee(s) think of. Don't expect to anticipate
everything. However, it is only a safety net if you *listen*.
The section on Coaching Questions has a reminder of the
problems that managers sometimes face with listening.

When you are *looking to the future* this is the major step as
you use this framework to test proposals which, necessarily,
are not yet detailed.

- You could be very clear in Step 1 but have little to
offer in Step 2; that is, you know the problem but
not the solution. You are saying *something* needs to
be done.

- In Step 2 all you can do is ask the employee to think
about it.

- When you use Step 4 to seek reactions the employee
will ask questions. By doing so he will learn more
about the problems of the change. He will be better
able to play his part in Step 5 and you will eventually be able to put together a complete proposal.

- This step may seem unnecessary if you are not
making a specific proposal. However, 'What do you
think?' can open up a list of things to be discussed,
researched and thought about. Bringing things into
the open can highlight unforeseen implications. And
all before any final decision has been made.

- Once a future change has been mentioned you can
ask, at intervals, 'Have you had any thoughts about
(the future change)?' If you raise no response you
can ask, 'Can you see any implications for your-self?'
In fact, that's a good question to ask at the outset, so
that you learn implications sooner rather than later.

> **5. Ask for their suggestions for (a) overcoming the problems** and (b) implementing the change, using a joint problem-solving approach.

When you switch into this two-part step you make the decision to move forward, towards your original objective (or an amended one) and towards an action plan.

Through careful listening in Step 4 you will have decided which concerns *must* be dealt with and which may safely be ignored. You may be able to summarize several concerns under one heading (or label); or you may have seen that fixing one thing will fix others and move you forward.

You can switch into this step with a restatement of the need for change or with a simple question like, 'How can we get over (this problem)?' You ask for suggestions to solve each problem brought forward from Step 4. These comprise any major hang-ups of a personal nature, (those to which you had no easy answer), and any new work problems.

Most people will see it as a point of pride to come up with a solution. If solutions are not complete you can build on them with your own ideas – this is the joint problem-solving approach; good positive teamwork.

If the employee has no ideas you can ask coaching questions (see the demonstrations for examples) or you can set a follow-up date to allow time for the employee to think through the problem. Try not to feel pressured to have all the answers yourself.

This step can seem almost magical because of the switch from negative to positive, and the lifting of pressure from your shoulders. But you *must* ask for ideas – and sometimes the employee is just waiting for that to happen.

Even if you personally cannot see your way round the problems remember that you are a team who can work together to either overcome the problems or eliminate them through the way the change is designed. Sometimes, however, if the employee has no hang-ups or problems, you may leave out 5(a) and move straight to 5(b).

> 5.  Ask for their suggestions for (a) overcoming the problems **and (b) implementing the change** using a joint problem-solving approach.

This part of Step 5 moves from consultation to making things happen. It asks the employee to make workable choices about timing, placing, etc.

- For a small change taking place at once you may ask, 'What's the best way of making it happen?' or, 'What's the next step then?'

- For a larger change you may ask, 'Can you work out a plan for implementation and come back to me?'

- For a future change you may say, 'Can you give some thought to implementation, but don't go firm yet as we're not sure what problems we will face.'

In each example the employee is able to get some control over their situation. This is important for their self-esteem in a change which *has* to happen.

If the employee has no ideas the boss has to ask the right questions, being still in the *joint* problem-solving mode.

Step 5(b) helps you to close the discussion with a follow-up date.

> 5.  Ask for their suggestions for (a) overcoming the problems and (b) implementing the change **using a joint problem-solving approach**

In joint problem-solving you use your experience to think of the *questions* which prompt the employee to come up with ideas – with you pulling together all the best bits. Often all you need is, 'What do you suggest?'

You can *build* on the good parts of a suggestion (and move away from the bad bits) with, eg 'Yes, *and* we could . . . ' If someone suggests an idea you don't like, you can ask for more ideas. Good ideas drive out bad ones.

*5. Ask for their suggestions for (a) overcoming the problems and (b) implementing the change **using a joint problem-solving approach** (continued)*

If you want the employee to understand *why* an idea is not so good ask about its *consequences*. This lets *them* work out why their idea has problems. You can then ask for new suggestions. Here are some examples of questions asking about consequences:

| Employee ideas | Questions to probe ideas for consequences |
|---|---|
| 'We ought to raise our prices.' | 'How would that affect sales?' |
| 'We ought to reduce our prices.' | 'How would that affect profits?' |
| 'We ought to offer a 10% discount.' | 'What extra sales do we need to pay for that?' |

Be ready to bring in your own ideas but only as necessary. In such cases, both in 5(a) and 5(b), you are better not making specific proposals because you might meet with the response, 'Yes but . . .'

Prefer, instead, to make suggestions on the lines of,

'What would happen if . . .' or

'How about . . .' or,

'What would you think of . . .?'

In that way you get the employee to think of ideas – even though the ideas are yours.

## Flexibility at the workplace

On a one-to-one basis you would use all five steps yourself but in a major change you may share out the work. You may use several media to handle Step 1. You may delegate Steps 2 and 3 to departmental heads and leave Steps 4 and 5 to be done collectively or individually in departments by first line supervisors. It is a flexible framework.

You may also ask your managers to go only up to and including 5(a) for the time being, before feeding back potential problems and areas of concern, some of which may be major hang-ups.

Now, of course, it starts to get complicated; which is an argument for having decisions made as low down in the hierarchy as possible.

## Notes

# HOW YOU CAN GO WRONG

Forewarned is forearmed so take a few minutes to see a few of the ways you can go wrong.

---

**(Consider objective, implications, alternatives and discretion.)**

---

☐ Failing to think through what you are trying to achieve, the objective, can mean that you get unnecessary argument and disagreement.

☐ If you don't think through implications of the change you could lose people's respect, and meet unexpected resistance.

☐ If you don't mention alternatives in Step 2 your employees may think of some. This puts you under pressure. If, on the other hand, you describe alternatives which you have *considered and discarded*, people may find it easier for to accept your plan. Ask, 'What options are there?' and try to generate at least three.

☐ If you don't use your discretion to clarify changes coming from above you this could leave you looking foolish in front of your people.

---

**1.   Explain the conditions which have brought about the need for change.**

---

☐ If you skip this step, or fail to cover it in sufficient depth, people may understand *what* they must do (from Step 2) without knowing *why*. If so, they cannot contribute alternative ideas.

Nor will they be able to cope well if things go wrong, because they lack the information they need to think for themselves.

---

---

**2. Explain the detail of the change and how it will affect the employee.**

---

☐ If you say, eg 'So what we're going to do is . . .' you may indicate that a 'proposal' is really a decision that is already made. This can cut people out of the decision-making process

Sometimes though, and only sometimes, it may be necessary. If that happens then Steps 2 and 3 will still help their understanding and using Steps 4 and 5 will get their participation.

☐ Suppose you carefully explain the detail of what people must do but fail to show how they will be affected; you could be seen as really inconsiderate. However, if you always emphasize *'My idea* is . . .' this shows you are still open to other ideas and you are less liable to criticism for shallow thinking.

---

**3. If applicable, include a practical demonstration or teach the employee how to carry out the new process.**

---

☐ If you do Step 3 badly, or not at all, you risk your employees having a different picture in their minds to the picture in yours. You also risk them failing. Do all you can to aid their understanding and acceptance. Their opinions and suggestions, coming next, will indicate how well they have understood.

---

**4. Ask the employee how he feels about the proposals; identify his major hang-ups and recognize any new problems.**

---

☐ Having gone through Steps 1, 2 and 3 you could now say, 'Right, I'll leave it with you,' and walk away. Or, 'Okay?' or 'Any problems?' in that tone of voice which forbids argument. Don't. Later, when things go wrong, the employee will say, 'I could have told you if you'd asked me'. This step is a safety net; it allows employees to raise matters you had not considered.

---

*4. Ask the employee how they feel about the proposals; identify their major hang-ups and recognise any new problems.Step 4 (Continued)*

☐ If an employee quickly agrees with your proposal, or has no questions, don't think you have done a super job of communicating. Perhaps the employee is wary of raising a question that could show how poor your thinking was. Ask open questions to get, and assess, the employee's reactions.

☐ You can appear to belittle objections and reservations by answering or dismissing them in a quickfire manner. You can lose out on valuable teamwork if you upset people in this way.

☐ If you get into too much detail discussing small hang-ups this will take up time and may crowd out later concerns. Ask, 'Is there anything else?' and look for major hang-ups. Then move to Step 5.

☐ You can put yourself under pressure by giving ill-considered answers. You will know this is happening when the employee has a new problem for every one that you try to deal with; your hasty answers raise these problems. If you ever feel under pressure see if you can adjourn – so that you both have time to think.

☐ Human nature means you don't *want* to hear too many problems, so you may appear annoyed or unsympathetic. Remind yourself that Step 4 is for getting facts and feelings, and putting labels on *those that matter*.

☐ Don't argue in this step. You may not like some of these unexpected concerns but simply ensure you understand them and be ready to carry them forward into the next step. That is where you can switch on people's creativity.

---

**5. Ask for their suggestions for (a) overcoming the problems**

---

☐ You can be so disappointed in Step 4, hearing problems for which you have no answer, that you despair and call it all off. Then you feel ineffectual and your self-esteem goes down. However, you have no monopoly on ideas, nor are you as expert in their field as your employees.

5. *Ask for their suggestions for (a) overcoming the problems (Continued)*

☐ Don't think, even subconsciously, that because *you* are without ideas then the employee must also be without. Ask, and you will be rewarded. If there should be no ideas right now, leave the employee to think some up; they're the experts.

> and **(b) implementing the change,** using a joint problem-solving approach.

☐ Bosses have been known to miss out this step and the employee goes away unsure what to do next. If you miss this you lose a chance for the employee to make a positive contribution. You also miss a chance to enhance their self-esteem. See the tips in 'Trying it out' later.

☐ Don't complicate the issue. This is a *framework* and with a simple routine change it may be enough to say, eg, 'Can you see to it?' Anything more complex requires the good teamwork encouraged by this framework.

> and (b) implementing the change,
> **using a joint problem-solving approach.**

☐ When you ask for suggestions *don't* go finding fault with them. Although the employee may just have been finding fault with your proposals this does *not* mean that you have to bite back and damage teamwork. Joint problem-solving means *using* their ideas to move forward. You have several options:

  ● Don't knock an idea by saying, 'That won't work, we've tried it.' Instead ask how they would avoid or overcome the problems you had previously.

  ● If you don't like a suggestion, just ask, 'Any other ideas?' The employee will come up with more ideas, the bad ones get forgotten.

  ● If an idea has good parts don't knock the bad parts. Eg the employee says, 'We could do A and B'. You believe A won't work so you just say, 'We could certainly do B, any other ideas?' Here you are agreeing with one part without accepting the other.

*and (b) implementing the change, **using a joint problem-solving approach.** (Continued)*

- Don't let an idea fall away if you can develop it. Eg the employee says, 'We could hit it with a seven pound hammer.' You reply, 'Yes, and we could hit it even harder with a twenty pound hammer'. Here you are *building on* an idea and the employee finds that acceptable.

- If the employee looks willing but clueless, don't jump in too quickly. You can ask people to *recall* what training or experience they have had which could relate to the problems to be solved. You can also ask who else might be able to help.

- If you come in too soon the employee may say, 'Yes, but . . .' to your ideas. If that happens you can ask. 'Well, what ideas do *you* have?' Only offer your own suggestions when you have tried really, *really* hard to get ideas from them.

- Finally, when there really are no suggestions from the employee don't *tell* them what to do. Seek their opinions on *your* suggestions. Even here you have to be careful with your words. If you said, 'Well, what you'd better do is use pink' you might get a 'Yes, but . . .' in reply. Better to *invite* the opinion rather than push the idea, eg 'How would it be if you used pink?'

> The plan agreed in this step may alter as the employee goes about the change, finding new problems and solving them – and leading to the right result.

# Notes

# COACHING QUESTIONS

You can gain further insights, and check your understanding of the preceding material, through the questions that follow. Please write your own answers before turning over.

1.  Think of a change recently introduced within your organization, *which proved difficult in some way.* Then, using the change framework on page 10, can you say why the difficulties occurred? And how they might have been avoided?

```



```

2.  Do you handle any changes, including routine instructions, where this framework of critical steps might *not* be appropriate? If so, what changes and why is the framework not appropriate?

```



```

3.  This book advocates sticking to the framework of critical steps and staying in sequence. What advantages can you see in sticking to the framework?

    Can you see any disadvantages?

```



```

# Comments

1. *About difficulties with a recent change. Why did the difficulties occur? How they might have been avoided?*

   You probably found that the people originating the change had missed out one or more steps from the Change framework; it is easy to handle Steps 4 and 5 badly.

   They may also have gone against one or more steps of the framework on Practical Leadership Skills

2. *Do you handle any changes where this framework of critical steps might not be appropriate? If so, what changes and why is the framework not appropriate?*

   There shouldn't be any, really. Even with routine instructions you give some background information. The instruction comes in Step 2. Step 3 may use a drawing or schedule or whatever. Step 4 may be as brief as, 'Any problems?' 5(a) may not be needed and 5(b) could be, 'I'll leave it with you' for a competent employee. About five seconds in all.

3. *This book advocates sticking to the framework of critical steps and staying in sequence. What advantages can you see in sticking to the framework? Can you see any disadvantages?*

   Advantages:

   (a) You have a foundation for planning and preparing, and for using aids.

   (b) You give information first which helps people to contribute later.

   (c) You always know where you are and how to move forward.

   Disadvantages:

   Only if you worry about the *next* step and thus mess up the current one. Use the card in the back cover to help you move through the framework one step at a time.

Don't forget to note your own thoughts in this panel

> **(Consider objective, implications, alternatives and discretion)**

## Questions on objectives

When people have a clear and agreed objective they can work towards it together. If an objective is not agreed, or is unclear, a great deal of effort can go to waste – with consequent loss of morale.

Objectives should:

(a) be measurable or verifiable, ie have criteria for success.

(b) be achievable but stretching.

(c) have a timescale.

This is not the place to go deeply into how and when objectives should be set but a couple of minutes on the following questions should prove worthwhile.

1. To what extent do you *think through* what you want to achieve from a discussion *before* you start into it? Circle one or more:

   Often      Always      Seldom      Now and again

   Superficially      In great depth      In some depth

2. To what extent do you clarify with your staff *why* you are wanting a change and what it is that you are trying to *achieve* with the change? Circle one or more:

   Often      Always      Seldom      Now and again

   Superficially      In great depth      In some depth

3. As an objective *for a discussion* is it reasonable to aim for, 'I just want them to agree to give it a go'?

            YES?          NO?

## Comments

1. *To what extent do you think through what you want to achieve from a discussion before you start into it?*

   The value of objectives is show in two famous quotations:

   > 'If you don't know where you're going you may end up somewhere else.'

   > 'He leapt on his horse and galloped off in all directions.'

2. *To what extent do you clarify with your staff what it is that you are trying to achieve with a change and why you want the change?*

   More relevant quotations on objectives:

   > 'If they know where they're going they can plot their own route to get there.'

   > 'Having lost sight of our objective we redoubled our efforts.'

3. *As an objective for a discussion is it reasonable to aim for, 'I just want them to agree to give it a go'?*

   Yes, this can be a very reasonable objective, especially where there is likely to be deep-seated resistance. Once people give something a go they are at least moving in the right direction; they are starting to dispel some of their fears and to gain confidence in their ability to do what is needed – or to handle any problems.

   And it is quite hard, even for someone against the change, to refuse to 'give it a go'.

# Questions on implications

When time is short for considering possible implications it is useful to have some idea of priorities. Here is a partial checklist. Please allocate the items to categories as follows:

A   Those implications which MUST be thought through.

B   Those implications you WANT to think through after you have finished with Category A items.

C   Those implications which it would be NICE to consider if you have time after the A and B items.

| | Possible implications to consider | Category |
|---|---|---|
| 1. | Whether anyone will lose in any way – in *their* eyes – by making the change. | |
| 2. | Whether any training will be needed, on-job or off-job. | |
| 3. | Whether any new methods, materials, machines have been tested so that you are introducing success, not failure. | |
| 4. | Whether people who may have to take on extra work are already fully loaded. | |
| 5. | Whether people will have to discard old skills learned over a long period. | |
| 6. | Whether anyone might be unable to make the change – for whatever reason. | |
| 7. | Any others you want to add? | |

# Comments

1. *Whether anyone will lose in any way – in their eyes – by making the change.*

   Probably a 'C' for senior managers who won't know people at the lower end. An 'A' for managers considering ALL people affected, eg, better productivity could mean people losing overtime, or redundancies. 'A' for junior managers communicating the change. 'B' is the average.

2. *Whether any training will be needed, on-job or off-job.*

   Training costs money. No training could well cost more. You might need time to prepare it. Start with an 'A'.

3. *Whether new methods, materials, machines have been tested so that you are introducing success, not failure.*

   New machinery, etc could be blamed for problems. It may be sensible to ask people involved to test it and help solve problems as part of training. Give this a 'B'.

4. *Whether people who may have to take on extra work are already fully loaded.*

   You would need reliable measures of current work, downtime, etc. People will tell you if it is tight, and they can do the measuring. This gets a 'B'.

5. *Whether people will have to discard old skills learned over a long period.*

   People discarding old skills lose something important. You'll have to convince them of the value of keeping up to date. This could be an 'A'.

6. *Whether anyone might be unable to make the change – for whatever reason.*

   Probably a 'C' unless there is a major leap in the competencies required. Appropriate training should fix up most people.

## Alternatives

With all but small or routine things you should try to generate more than one way of going about change. You may come up with only two ways but one of them can become the contingency plan if something goes wrong.

Even better is to generate several alternatives with your team. The final way of going about things might then be a combination from several of them.

Failure to generate alternative courses of action can have serious consequences.

## 'There is no alternative' – exercise

Under the heading of Alternatives will you please take a few minutes on this small task? The reason for it will become clear shortly.

At the local sports centre there were 167 entrants for the tennis annual knockout competition. At the end of it Jackie Smith won the trophy.

The question is, 'How many matches had to be played before Jackie emerged the winner?' (Each match was the best of three sets and you are looking for how many matches were *played.*)

You can work on your answer here.

Comments are overleaf but please finish the task first, or go as far as you can.

---

# Answer

People take one of two approaches to this question.

One is to work backwards, ie there is a winner from the final which takes two people. Semi-finals make two more matches (3 in all) and two more people (now 4 in all). The quarter finals are four matches (now 7 matches) and four more people (now 8), and so on up to 128 people with 39 left over. And all 39 have to play a match to join the 128.

The other way is to start with a figure of 167 but needing 128 to go into the second round. The 39 odd people (167 minus 128) play 39 others in 39 matches to produce 39 winners whilst 89 people have a bye. 39 winners plus 89 with byes gives 128. This drops to 64 in 64 more matches, to 32 in 32 more, to 16 in 16 more, to 8 in 8 more, then to 4, then to 2 and to a final winner in the one last match.

Working all this out takes time and you can have several false starts. But there is an alternative way of going about it.

|  |
|---|
| *39* |
| *64* |
| *32* |
| *16* |
| *8* |
| *4* |
| *2* |
| *1* |
| ——— |
| *166* |
| ——— |

> There has be a loser in every match so, with 167 starting off, there will be 166 losers.
> This means there are 166 matches.

That didn't take quite so long did it? The moral of the story is that we become used to certain ways of doing things and may be in danger of never thinking in any other way.

That's bad enough but a bigger danger is that because WE can see no alternative we convince ourselves that *there is no alternative!* Ours is the ONLY way! We forget that others may have different ideas for getting where we want to be.

We can also forget that other people may have different ideas for *where* we ought to be going in response to the conditions that have brought about the need for change. They may think a different *objective* is more appropriate. All this is good reason for starting to discuss the *need* for change before getting locked into a single idea or being rigid on the shape of the objective. It is also a good argument for coaching; more about this later.

# Questions on discretion

1. Imagine you have a change imposed on you from above. Your boss doesn't explain *why* the change has to take place but tells you *what* to do. You don't agree with it but have to pass it on to your people.

   Which of the following plans is most likely to get good results from them?

   A. Although you do not fully understand the reasons for the change this hardly matters because you have no choice about implementing it. So you tell your people that the change comes from on high and you have no option but to ask them to go through with it.

   B. Although you do not fully understand the *reasons* for the change you explain the *detail* of the change and how each employee is affected.

   C. Not fully understanding the reasons for the change you ask the boss for a full explanation and discussion, before you talk to your own people.

Your answer:

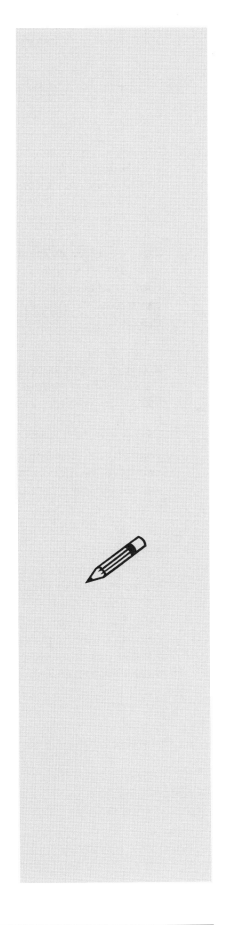

Comments are overleaf.

## Comments

1. Which plan is most likely to get good results from your team?

   A. *Although you do not fully understand the reasons for the change this hardly matters because you have no choice about implementing it. So you tell your people that the change comes from on high and you have no option but to ask them to go through with it.*

      This would be an abdication of responsibility on your part. If you don't understand a change well enough to adequately explain it to your people, how can you show your own commitment in order to gain theirs?

   B. *Although you do not fully understand the reasons for the change you explain the detail of the change and how each employee is affected.*

      This means you really can't take much responsibility yourself, nor can you show your commitment – if you have any. You may have a hard time when you are not able to answer legitimate questions from employees.

   C. *Not fully understanding the reasons for the change you ask the boss for a full explanation and discussion, before you talk to your own people.*

      Only here are you really using your discretion. If you can explain the "why" to your people you are in a better position to show commitment and work with them towards an appropriate plan of action.

Have you ever seen managers working to Plan A or Plan B? What seemed to be the effect of that?

A further question on discretion.

2.  Some changes have to happen, and you can't argue, but where would you see yourself as likely to have some choice or discretion among the following?

    Please place a ✓ in one column or the other.

| Area of possible discretion | Some choice | No choice |
|---|---|---|
| Whether or not to raise any problems you foresee. | | |
| How to resolve any problems you foresee. | | |
| Timing of implementation of the change. | | |
| The exact method for implementing the change. | | |
| Who should be involved in making it happen. | | |
| Whether you may resolve unforeseen problems yourself or refer them to someone else. | | |
| Whether you should give your staff the reasoning behind the change and how it should be done. | | |

Comments are overleaf.

## Comments

| Some choice or no choice? | |
|---|---|
| Whether or not to raise any problems you foresee. | You should have been able to tick 'Some choice' for every item. If you didn't, that may say something about *your perception* of your boss's trust in you. |
| How to resolve any problems you foresee. | |
| Timing of implementation of the change. | |
| The exact method for implementing the change. | |
| Who should be involved in making it happen. | |
| Whether you may resolve unforeseen problems yourself or refer them to someone else. | |
| Whether you should give your staff the reasoning behind the change and how it should be done. | |

Now, having looked at the thinking and planning stage, let's move on to the discussion itself.

> **1. Explain the conditions which have brought about the need for change.**

Take a minute or two to consider possible changes before they become urgent.

1.  What conditions are bringing about, or may bring about, a need for change in your organization?  Consider materials, technology, customers, competitors, government action, and anything else relevant to your industry. Consider also how any changes within the organization will impact on your own department.

Having thought about them, you can raise these issues now, in good time, thus getting others to think about them.

2.  With whom should you be discussing these things in order to get their contribution?

3.  With whom should you be discussing these things in order to gauge their likely support for any future proposals you may make?

Continued over-
leaf. Use the
margins to
expand on your
thoughts about
change in your
organization.

4. With whom should you be discussing these things in order to show that you are already thinking about the issues and could therefore be consulted regarding them?

___

**2. Explain the detail of the change and how it will affect the employee.**

1. Think about one change which you would like to bring about (it doesn't matter right now if it is not in your power). Who is likely to be affected, and how?

| Who is likely to be affected? | And how? (Plus and minus) | (Leave until later) |
|---|---|---|
|  |  |  |

Comments on this will come later.

2. *Explain the detail of the change and how it will affect the employee. (Continued)*

2. You could ask people what they think about the *idea* of a change before you work out a detailed, firm proposal to put to them. This may, or may not, be a good idea. What do you think – and why?

3. If there are ways in which a person may lose out from a change, ie some minuses, should you mention these minuses or leave people to find out for themselves? What is your reasoning?

Comments on are on the next page.

# Comments

1. *Think about one change which you would like to bring about (it doesn't matter right now if it is not in your power). Who is likely to be affected, and how?*

Comments on this come later in the book.

2. *You could ask people what they think about the idea of a change before you work out a detailed, firm proposal to put to them. This may, or may not, be a good idea. What do you think – and why?*

With some changes, firm proposals often require people to make up their minds and take a position. However, *raising an idea*, or the problem causing the need for change, invites comment without people having to take a firm position. This can be a good idea when you want to obtain views, and/or assess likely support.

You can also hear about likely obstacles to a change *before* you get down to the hard work of thinking everything through.

3. *If there are ways in which a person may lose out from a change, ie some minuses, should you mention these minuses or leave people to find out for themselves? What is your reasoning?*

There are three things to consider here.

(a) What will happen to the trust between you and your people if they were left to find the nasties, or reason them out, for themselves?

(b) If you did know the minuses would it not be sensible to find the counter-balancing pluses so that you could mention both? Or/and, if you know the minuses you can decide if you want to alter the detail so the minuses don't occur.

(c) Either way, do you want to be in a negotiating situation about the pluses and minuses, or not?

Rehearsing this step, and people's questions, helps you to see some of the implications of the change. Then you can consider who may help in the early thinking about it.

**3. If applicable, include a practical demonstration or teach the employee how to carry out the new process.**

You may be well into the following skills already, but let's check how effective you think you are. For each skill mark your position on the scale provided.

1 = 'I am 100% on top of this.'

2 = 'I am up to date in most aspects.'

3 = 'I need to brush up on some aspects.'

4 = 'I need a good grounding in this.'

Handling a presentation.

Making flipcharts, transparencies, computer presentations.

Teaching a new task or process.

Knowing training or other organizations which can help.

What action should you take, if any, to improve your ability within this step? Note your answers in the margin.

*3. If applicable, include a practical demonstration or teach the employee how to carry out the new process. (Continued)*

Here are a few ways of giving a practical demonstration – a term which covers anything at all that will help the employee to form a picture in his mind of what is required and/or why it is required. Will you please think back over your own experience and add your own ideas to the list.

1. A few figures on the back of an envelope.

2. The brochure in the second demonstration, plus joining instructions and the performance review form.

3. The leaflets in the fourth demonstration.

4. The overtime booking sheet for next week in the fifth demonstration.

5. The sketch in the sixth demonstration of the jobs and processes.

6. Demonstrating how a new piece of equipment works.

7. Taking someone to another business to see a new process there.

_____

_____

_____

_____

> **4. Ask the employee how he feels about the proposals; identify his major hang-ups and recognize any new problems.**

This step, remember, is a safety net – where you catch the things you didn't think of yourself. But only if you listen. Check below how you are doing on that skill.

Here are several BLOCKS TO GOOD LISTENING. See if any of them apply to you sometimes. If so please mark them.

| BLOCKS TO GOOD LISTENING | Tick if it applies |
|---|---|
| 1. *Rehearsing your reply* while the other person is speaking – so that you don't hear the rest. | |
| 2. *Being hurried* and listening on the run. | |
| 3. *Hearing only what you want to hear* and screening out the unwelcome bits. | |
| 4. *Other things on your mind*, so you can't give your full attention to the speaker. | |
| 5. *Disagreeing* with the other person's point of view (back to [1] above). | |
| 6. *Evaluating* what is being said, ie getting hung-up on the early words and not hearing the rest. | |
| 7. *Feeling pressured* that you must have an answer or decision at once (back to [1] above). | |
| 8. *Searching for the next question.* This puts you under pressure so that you cannot listen to the last response. Thus you misunderstand and come under more pressure – now or later. | |

**Action**  If you marked any blocks to good listening which sometimes apply to you, please note in the margin how you will overcome them.

*4.   Ask the employee how he feels about the proposals; identify his major hang-ups and recognize any new problems. (continued)*

## Think again

Look back to page 98,  those people who may be affected by the change you would like to make, and put yourself in *their* shoes. Think of what *they* see themselves as losing. Think of the obstacles which *they* are likely to see. These things are the hang-ups and new problems they are likely to raise when you get to this step.

*Make a note* of these things in the third column on page 98. If you have well and truly thought yourself into their shoes you may find that column 3 items are different to your thoughts in column 2. Are they, in any way?

Now imagine – in graphic detail – that these people are actually working in the new way. This will give you some idea of the training and/or practical demonstrations needed in Step 3.

5. **Ask for his suggestions for (a) overcoming the problems** and (b) implementing the change, using a joint problem-solving approach.

This asks you to look at how different employees may react to your ideas. Visualize talking *separately* to two employees of yours, X and Y, who are *very different to each other.*

Imagine you ask for suggestions to overcome a problem *and then realize that you have an idea for solving it.* Without waiting for their ideas, you say to the employee, 'What you can do is . . .', so you push your own idea.

How do you think each employee might react? Which of the following would be closest to employee X, and which would be closest to employee Y? Note their initials if you wish.

| | The employee's reaction to 'What you can do is . . .' | X ( ) | Y ( ) |
|---|---|---|---|
| A | 'Well, okay, if that's what you want, that's what I'll do.' | | |
| B | 'Yes, but if we did that, what about the (whatitsname)?' | | |
| C | 'Yes, and if we did that we could also . . .' | | |
| D | 'That's a good idea boss, I think we should do that.' | | |
| E | 'I can't see that working, boss.' | | |

Comments are on the next page.

## Comments

Reactions will vary depending on the employee and, just as important, on how you normally handle them.

| | 'What you can do is . . .' | Comments |
|---|---|---|
| A | 'Well, okay, if that's what you want, that's what I'll do.' | Here the employee feels dictated to by the boss. You then need to *ask a question* to properly involve the employee, eg 'Well, what ideas do you have?' |
| B | 'Yes, but if we did that, what about the . . . ?' | People can ignore the good parts of an idea and home in on the 2% that might cause a problem. Annoying. Try to get agreement that 98% of the idea is okay and then ask for ideas for solving the problem they have identified. |
| C | 'Yes, and if we did that we could also . . .' | Here the employee is building on your idea, a very constructive piece of behaviour that keeps the discussion moving forward. |
| D | 'That's a good idea boss, I think we should do that.' | This might be as passive as (A) above, but certainly appears more positive. The employee could be encouraging *you* to come up with ideas – a reversal of roles! If you are in 5(a) get his involvement in 5(b). |
| E | 'I can't see that working, boss.' | This is nice and honest so be careful about your tone of voice when you ask, 'Why not?' or the employee may never disagree with you again – which is an important part of effective teamwork. However, asking 'Why not?' does get more information about the problem and leads to more ideas from one or both of you. |

(A) and (B) above are typical reactions if you put forward your own ideas *before* you get theirs. (C), (D) and (E) need good team players so, again, try for their ideas first.

5. Ask for his suggestions for (a) overcoming the problems **and (b) implementing the change,** using a joint problem-solving approach.

## Giving choice, getting ideas

When a change *has* to happen Step 5(b) gives the employee some choice instead of no choice. It maintains self-esteem by inviting ideas on, eg, the next step, who will do what, where and when, how, etc, etc. They will move forward more positively when they can influence what happens next.

Think now about changes that you typically make and note just three ways in which you could offer choice and discretion to an employee. An example is provided.

Look at the demonstrations again, if you wish.

a. 'When could you take delivery?'

b.

c.

d.

> 5. Ask for his suggestions for (a) overcoming the problems and (b) implementing the change **using a joint problem-solving approach**.

Joint problem-solving is an important skill requiring a fine balance.

Imagine that you, yourself, put forward an idea to your boss, to handle a problem that you have seen with a change that he has proposed. Imagine that the boss immediately rejects your idea as unworkable.

Using your experience, think how you might respond. Note your likely response in the box please.

When you have finished see how you compare with what is below.

Some possible responses:

You could get angry with the boss.

You might keep arguing to make your idea work.

You might start finding fault with his solution.

Or you might opt out of the discussion with an, "Okay, if that's what you want."

Would your people react in the same way if you handled their ideas badly?

Some bosses may involve their people in changes either too little or too late; because they have little confidence in them, or because they confuse participation with permissiveness, or both

## Last coaching question

What guidelines would you use to get your people participating but without your being permissive? Take a few minutes over this if necessary.

Comments are on the next page.

## Comments

*What guidelines would you use to get your people participating but without your being permissive?*

Naturally, you could use this framework for Overcoming Resistance to Change.

There is less chance of your being permissive without realizing it because, after you have gone through Step 4, you have to decide whether to move forward or not. And whether or not to amend the objective of the change itself or of the discussion.

These are deliberate choices. If you were permissive, and giving in, you should know it.

One thing to remember about 'participation' is that it *does not mean* that your people ought to have their own way.

When people express their opinions and make suggestions they are *contributing* towards a decision but *you* remain accountable for it. This is participation – and good teamwork.

This framework helps you to take account of other people's views whilst remaining in control of the discussion.

The framework of Practical Leadership Skills is another useful set of guidelines.

> If you wrote down separate guidelines of your own you will probably find that, although the words may be different, the meaning will be much the same as the framework for Overcoming Resistance to Change; with some or all of the framework of Practical Leadership Skills thrown in. Look back to pages 10 and 12.

# EXCEPTIONAL SITUATIONS

## ('Yes, but . . .' and 'What if . . . ?')

If you think the demonstrations seemed to go well you have to remember:

## ACTION ➡ ➡ ➡ REACTION

- If you handle people well they usually respond well.
- If you listen well they'll contribute.
- If you are positive it is hard for them to be negative.

The whole thrust of this framework, with the framework for Practical Leadership Skills, is positive. However, people don't always behave as you want so some possible awkward situations, listed below, are expanded in the following pages.

1. 'Suppose they don't agree with the reason for change?'

2. 'What if they are divided about what we ought to do?'

3. 'What if there are real disadvantages for them?'

4. 'If one complains they all start.'

5. 'What if they persist in finding fault?'

6. 'What if they come up with bad ideas in Step 4 or 5?'

7. 'Suppose they really dig in?'

8. 'Yes, but they attack my ideas as soon as I speak.'

9. 'Yes, but some people ask silly questions.'

10. 'What if we get opposition from outside the team?'

11. 'What if my ideas are better than theirs?'

12. 'What if they refuse?'

13. A pleasant exception.

## 1. 'Suppose they don't agree with the reason for change?'

Either *they* have thought about the future better than you or you did not give a thorough explanation of the conditions which have brought about the need for change.

In the first case ask for their forecasts and ask questions to test their thinking. In the second you have to decide if you should stop now and organize yourself better for another try in the future. Or fill in the gaps you left in Step 1.

## 2. 'What if they are divided about what we ought to do?'

This may happen if you have not clarified what the change is expected to achieve; people then argue for their own ideas. Take the example of two people jointly buying a house and trying to decide between three houses which seem suitable. Unless they *first* decide what they want from a house it is difficult to rationally compare the choices.

Once they have discussed, agreed and listed their requirements they can check each house against that list.

So, if you have disagreement about *how* to achieve an objective, set aside for the moment the ideas which are competing for attention. Ask what you want to achieve. Break that down into measures of success (or decision criteria). If you do this you will often find that one course of action emerges as the clear winner. However, if the decision is close then you have to choose. Everyone will have participated but *you* decide because you are accountable for the team's output.

## 3. 'What if there are real disadvantages for them?'

First check if there really, *really* is a need for change. If NO, forget it. If YES you should have a convincing argument, to which you can then add something like:

> 'So if we want to stay in business . . .'
> 'So if we want to remain competitive . . .'
> 'So if we want to keep our jobs . . .'

Be careful with the additional remarks on the previous page. They may sound like a veiled threat, even though we all know that having a job is a good thing.

## 4. 'If one complains they all start.'

You may have seen how people can sink into a morass of problem-*finding*, and how others in a meeting can join in! You may also have seen how managers can take the "easy" way out of this situation by accepting the problems as insurmountable. Then they come to a halt, or accept an unsatisfactory compromise.

The solution comes when you move into Step 5(a), and switch the employees' energy from problem-stating to problem-*solving*. Most people in a team will be waiting for you to do this.

## 5. 'What if they persist in finding fault?'

This may happen if employees are testing the boss's resolve. Or an employee may be dead against a change.

When you move into Step 5, after working hard in Step 4, you effectively *require* them to make the change. But they can become committed through helping to solve the problems they raised.

You can also ask how they would achieve the same *overall* objective. Then, given that you have conveyed a convincing need for change, they have to 'go positive'. Be ready to use any good ideas!

## 6. 'What if they come up with bad ideas in Step 4 or 5?'

This may happen if you have not agreed criteria for success (see the example of the houses in Situation 2 on the previous page). You can put these criteria into Step 1 by saying, eg 'So we need something that reduces costs by at least 10%, it has to be a sustainable saving, and it must be quick to implement. My idea (now into Step 2) was . . . '

Continued overleaf.

In the face of bad ideas you may sometimes have to repeat what you are trying to achieve and ask how their ideas contribute, eg 'How much will that cut costs?' This kind of coaching question gets people thinking better.

## 7. 'Suppose they really dig in?'

If the employee's concerns weigh so strongly against your proposals that your original objective no longer seems achievable you may adjourn in Step 4. This allows time for you and your employee(s) to think things over. Using your discretion you have to decide whether or not to change your overall objective.

## 8. 'Yes, but they attack my ideas as soon as I speak.'

Acknowledge their comments to show you are listening, but ask them to hold questions until later. Make sure you set out your stall properly (see the demonstrations).

Caution.     If you believe a change *must* happen you may put a lot of effort into it and thus be quite forceful. Because *you* can see clearly the need for change you may be intolerant of apparent scepticism. But resistance is legitimate. Step 4 is for listening, exploring and inquiring, *not* for a battle of wits. Use that step to get the employee on your side.

## 9. 'Yes, but some people ask silly questions.'

Some questions may cause you to think that people weren't listening as you went through Steps 1 to 3, and this may make you angry. However, people think faster than you can speak so their thoughts crowd out your words. Hence the 'stupid' questions when you have just been giving the answers.

People will raise questions about matters which seem trivial to you. Take them at face value and acknowledge the speakers' expressed concerns. Give answers where you can, or involve them in finding the solutions.

It's worth repeating that one way to aid understanding is to show how the employee is NOT affected. This can reduce distracting thoughts and 'stupid' questions.

## 10. 'What if we get opposition from outside the team?'

This takes you back to the planning stage. Look at discretion and implications, and who else is affected. Ask yourself who can help, and who has relevant ideas or experience.

## 11. 'What if my ideas are better than theirs?'

They would need to be significantly better. If there is not much between your ideas and theirs be prepared to take a risk with their ideas. Set a follow-up date in the *near* future if you wish to see that they are not going wrong.

Remember, people run better with their own ideas.

Remember, too, that by *building* on their ideas – without distorting them – you both win; joint problem-solving.

## 12. 'What if they refuse?'

Find out their thinking and remember that people often have good reasons for resistance, reasons which they may find difficult to state. For example:

- One employee refused a generous redundancy package because he was running a very profitable racket at the expense of his employer's customers.

- The present way gives them overtime or other perks.

- They believe they could work themselves out of a job.

- They believe the change is too complicated, etc.

You can repeat that the change *has* to happen, and give them time to think through the problems they have raised. You can ask what will happen if we don't change.

Continued overleaf.

You can ask for other ways of achieving the objective. You can ask yourself if you want to modify your objective.

The last resort is to ask them to give it a go; a grudging, 'All right then,' is better than insubordination. If refusal persists you have to ask yourself if the change is really worth the hassle of pushing it through.

If the change is still worthwhile, and if someone is not prepared to change you may decide that you cannot continue to employ them. If so, see the book on *Changing Unacceptable Performance*.

## 13.   A pleasant exception.

People can often see when something ought to be changed. They may not give it the necessary thought or take the initiative, but that's where leaders come in.

In cases like that you will probably hear people saying, 'We've been wondering when you'd do something', or 'Well, we couldn't go on like this for much longer.'

That will not stop them finding fault with your detailed proposal, or wanting to improve on it. They may even have well-formed ideas of their own. But there is no argument about the need for change.

It is sensible to always regard your own proposal as a first draft; and first drafts usually get changed.

# TRYING IT OUT

## ONE STEP AT A TIME,
## THEN ALL TOGETHER

You can build up your skills on the job by trying the steps one at a time and then combining them. You can ask your boss for advice if you wish. You can rehearse using the whole framework with a colleague or your boss, or a trainer. There is provision for this at the end of this section.

People learn by *doing,* by reflecting on how it went, and by working out how to improve. So please *plan* to use this framework, and *carry out your plan.*

By now you know the framework is sensible so stick with it; then you will know which step you are in at any time in a discussion. If you find that you have lost your way it will probably be because you are not moving from step to step in a deliberate fashion.

Give the planning stage the time that the change deserves. You can then prepare steps 1, 2 and 3; so do so, even if only briefly. The better you prepare, the better it will go.

The important thing is to try it out; don't just read about it and hope you will somehow remember in the future. Try it out, learn from the experience and try again.

The chances are that you will get most things mostly right first time round. If you experience any difficulties you probably won't need much help to get over them. The tips that follow are therefore very small ones.

> **1.**     **Explain the conditions which have brought about the need for change.**

When giving instructions, or asking for help with a change, start small and in three stages.

## Action Plan

a. Try using the following phrase *or something similar:*

'I'm going to ask if you can help me.'

That usually gets people listening and more receptive to your words.

b. Then, for any change which is more than a small routine matter, try out the following phrase, *or something similar:*

'Let me give you some background, then the detail, and then I'll ask how you feel about it.'

One expression for this approach is, "Setting out your stall."

c. After "setting out your stall" take the trouble to explain *why* you are making the request; in other words, explain the conditions which have brought about the need for the person to do something they may otherwise not expect to do.

Finally, *be clear* why you want the person to do whatever it is. Be sure how important it is and how urgent it is. These things will obviously influence what you say in Step 1.

You'll find that this step sometimes takes only a few seconds. You may also notice that people are more ready to listen to you, better able to understand what you want of them, and happier to go along with you.

## Result

How did it work for you?

How do you need to improve?

If you had any difficulty why not read through this material again?

| 2. | **Explain the detail of the change and how it will affect the employee.** |
| --- | --- |

Below are examples of a person switching from Step 1 into Step 2.

| | | |
| --- | --- | --- |
| a. | 'So what I want you to do is . . . and it's just for the next hour or so.' | This is a clear instruction, an order, and very firm. It puts a limit on the period of change. |
| b. | 'So what I'm asking you to do is . . .' | This is an instruction too, but couched in terms which allow the employee to participate more easily. |
| c. | 'So my idea was that we . . .' | Using 'my idea' indicates that the speaker is open to other ideas and is offering a "first draft" that can be changed. |
| d. | 'So what I thought was . . .' | This is similar to (c). |
| e. | 'So that's the problem we have to deal with. I'm asking you to think about it and see what you can come up with.' | There is no detail explained. Instead, 'how it will affect the employee' is by having to think about the detail. |

## Action Plan

For each of your own discussions on change, no matter how small, decide which type of phrase best fits your objective for the discussion and try using your own version of it with the appropriate detail.

## Result

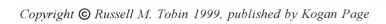

How did it work for you?

How do you need to improve?

If you occasionally missed small details do you need to think things through better beforehand? Or note key words?

On the other hand, if you spent too much time working out the detail remember that you have a team to support you, and they can fill in what you miss out. That is what Steps 4 and 5 are for. Try to find the right balance.

> **3. If applicable, include a practical demonstration or teach the employee how to carry out the new process.**

Here are several ways of giving a practical demonstration (*anything* which aids understanding). Tick those which are most suitable to your usual situations of change.

1. Making a rough sketch with a pencil or pen.
2. Showing a technical drawing, a schedule or list.
3. Using a chalkboard, flipchart, overhead projector or slide projector.
4. Using a video or film.
5. Using a scale model.
6. Taking the employee somewhere else to see a process. Other ideas (please specify):

_____

And here are several ways of teaching the employee how to carry out a new process as quickly as possible.

1. The employee learns by sitting with a co-worker who carries out the process and explains it. Then the learner tries it.
2. The employee learns in a group from a trainer, practises and gets feedback.
3. The employee learns by carrying out written instructions.
4. The employee learns from watching a video.
5. The employee learns by using a computer based training programme.
6. The employee learns by reading or watching material and answering questions on the material (like this book).
7. The employee learns by trial and error.
8. Learning in some other way (please specify)

_____

## Action Plan

> Plan to use one or more of these methods for Step 3 next time you have to bring in a change, even if it is only a small one.

## Result

How did it go at work?



How do you need to improve?



Were employees pleased to see that you had taken some care over Step 3?

> **4.** **Ask the employee how he feels about the proposals; identify his major hang-ups and recognize any new problems.**

Employee responses can fall into three categories:

a.   After you ask how they feel about the change, they respond with something like, 'No problem' and you know this is very likely to be true.

b.   After you ask how they feel, they respond with something like 'No problem' and you are amazed to hear this as you thought the change was something outside their experience.

c.   After you ask, the employee responds with questions, eg, 'Yes, but . . . ', 'What about . . .?',  or 'What if  . . .?'

## Action Plan

With your next three proposals, even if they seem to be well accepted, ask, 'Can you see any problems with that?' or something similar. Then *deliberately decide* how to handle each response:

●   for (a) above, just move forward to Step 5(b) – implementation.

●   for (b) think back to what you said in Step 2 and probe their understanding with *open* questions, eg 'What do you think of the X move?' (This is better than a closed question like, 'Do you see any problems with the X move?' which may get another 'No problem.')

●   for (c) welcome these signs of involvement; *listen actively.* Answer only those things which are *easy* to answer *and* where your answers form part of necessary but omitted information. Note any other things for Step 5.

## Result

How did it go at work?




How do you need to improve?

Reflecting, questioning, probing, and probably taking notes, help you to check employees' understanding. If you felt pressurized to think up answers, don't be; Step 5 is for finding solutions. Use Step 4 to focus on active listening.

4. Ask the employee how he feels about the proposals; identify his major hang-ups and recognize any new problems. (continued)

A really good way to listen well, and to show it, is to summarize what the speaker is saying. One definition of good listening, and summarizing, is:

> You should be able to express the speaker's ideas in your own words – *to his or her satisfaction* – before you react.

Here are some ways to start into summarizing:

- 'So what you're saying is . . . (have I got you right?)'

- 'Are you saying that . . . '

- 'If I understand you correctly . . .'

- 'You seem to be saying . . . '

If you would like to work on this critical skill, try rolling these phrases round your tongue. Listen to what other people say and devise your own phrases.

## Action Plan

> Note here the one or two 'summarizing openers' that you will try out. Then use them whenever you want to ensure that you have understood someone – and where you want them to know that you have been listening carefully.

## Result

How did your phrases work for you?

How do you need to improve?

Did you find that people organize their thoughts better if they know you are listening?

> 5. **Ask for his suggestions for (a) overcoming the problems** and (b) implementing the change, using a joint problem-solving approach.

This step moves you forward in two quite separate stages.

Switching from Step 4 (the listening step) into 5(a) should be done quite deliberately. Here are several ways of making the switch. You may like to practise using these phrases or something similar, and note your own:

a. 'Well, it's something that has to happen, so let's see what can be done about this problem of . . . What do you think?'

b. 'We need some more thinking on this. Let's go through my notes and put our heads together. The first thing is . . .'

c. 'The major problem seems to be . . . How do you think that can be dealt with?'

d. _____

_____

e. _____

_____

## Action Plan

> Work on this switch from listening to problem-solving. In *any* sort of discussion focus on each problem in turn and seek suggestions to solve it. Avoid putting your own ideas in first.
>
> The challenge is to draw solutions from the employee, and build on them.

## Result

How did it go at work?




How do you need to improve?




Did ideas come mainly from you – or from the employee?

Did they delight you with their problem-solving abilities?

Did employees find fault with ideas from you? If so, was that because you were too quick with your ideas?

5.  Ask for his suggestions for (a) overcoming the
    problems **and (b) implementing the change,** using a
    joint problem-solving approach.

After working to overcome problems one can forget to
actually make things happen, which is often the objective of
the discussion. So, whether or not there are problems to
overcome in Step 5(a), *moving things forward* in Step 5(b),
also has to be done in a studied way.

There are various ways you can do this. How would you
feel about some of the following? Would you like to run
through them and note your own?

a.  'What's the next step, do you think?'

b.  'What is the best place/time/way to make a start?'

c.  'Are you ready to give it a go?'

d.  'Will you draw up an action programme?'

e.  _____

    _____

f.  _____

    _____

## Action Plan

Work at giving the employee some sort of choice in
5(b) by asking for suggestions. Note your preferred
ways here.

## Result

How did it go at work?




How do you need to improve?




Did you find that Step 5(b) helps to bring the discussion to an end?

And that moving towards implementation can be a face-saver for an employee who appeared resistant?

5.  Ask for his suggestions for (a) overcoming the problems and (b) implementing the change, **using a joint problem-solving approach**.

The best role for you is to help the employee come up with ideas by asking coaching questions. When you point out that they are the experts, or that they are nearest to the problems, you also enhance their self-esteem.

At the same time recognize that the change may create problems for the employee and be ready to come in where you have experience that they don't; it may not be sensible to ask coaching questions if they clearly have no relevant learning or experience.

If you do have to put in your own suggestions choose your words carefully, eg:

- 'Have you thought about . . . ?'

- 'Have you ever tried . . . ?

- 'What I've found useful is . . . How would that be here?'

## Action Plan

> Seeking suggestions, building on them and clarifying them are things you should try out whenever you can. Only as a last resort should you **offer** your suggestions, and ask for the employee's opinions on them.
>
> Try the phrases above or something similar. Note here what you will try.

## Result

How did it go at work?

How do you need to improve?

Did you enjoy approving *their* action plan instead of seeking their approval for yours?

Did that actually enhance the quality of the discussion?

Did you like the teamwork in joint problem-solving?

If you found resistance to your ideas, were they framed as *suggestions*, ('How would it be if . . . ?') or as *instructions* ('What you should do is . . .')?

## Final Action Plan

1. Review your successes and also where you need to work harder. Give yourself credit for the things you have done well.

   Note them here so you can build on them.

2. What is the *one* skill area that could make a lot of difference? Note it here and work on it. Seek help if necessary.

# REHEARSAL EXERCISE

A rehearsal pulls together the skills you have been trying out separately. The questions overleaf will help you prepare for a discussion about bringing in change.

If necessary, agree with your boss a project for bringing in a change somewhere in your area of responsibility. S/he may give advice and follow up. If you don't personally have a current change situation try, for this rehearsal, to adapt one from something happening elsewhere in the organization. The aim of this exercise is to practise your skills.

Think through the change and write relevant information in the spaces provided on page 136 and 137.

You can practise handling the situation by asking a colleague (or boss or trainer) to take the employee role opposite you. Brief them with the information on page 137.

In the discussion you may want, perhaps using page 136, to make notes like those shown in the example on page 138.

After your practice ask for feedback on how you followed the steps in this framework and the skills in the Practical Leadership Skills framework. Ask the 'employee' how he felt about the way you handled him.

If you tape record the practice the playback lets you better understand employee feedback. You can also reflect on how your behaviour would have influenced *you* if you had been in the "employee" seat.

You may find it useful to repeat the practice, trying different ways of following the steps, and with the 'employee' being more difficult, or raising different problems. You may also wish to re-read one or more demonstrations before you repeat (or attempt) this exercise.

If you do ask the employee to be more difficult you should still follow the framework (just concentrate more) so that you are controlling your own behaviour rather than reacting to theirs.

NB The next two pages are the only ones that you may photocopy. You can thus rehearse as many discussions as you like, especially important ones.

# Your own viewpoint (as boss/leader)

Think of a change that you intend to make, or would like to make if you had the power. It should be something which the 'employee' can relate to. Then consider, and note below:

What is the overall objective?

What do you want to achieve in the discussion itself (action, think it over, test the water, what)?

What implications do these objectives have?

What alternatives have you considered?

What discretion do you have?

1. What is the background to the change, (why is it needed), how *strong* is the need?

2. What is the detail – of the change itself, and how is the employee affected (+ or -)? How is the employee NOT affected?

3. What could you show or do to help the employee understand (a sketch, schedule, etc)? Will there be any training?

4.                                        ➔        5(a)

5 (b)

What might be a good follow-up date?
And for what purpose?

# The employee's viewpoint

This page is to brief the stand-in 'employee' with whom you will practise.

6.  The 'employee' is a _____ (job title/s)

7.  The change is about: _____

8.  What personal hang-ups may the employee have in this situation? What work problems might they mention? What questions may they ask?

9.  What ideas may the *employee* have for overcoming problems where you have no ready answer.

---

### For the stand-in 'employee'

The aim of this exercise is for the 'boss' to practise using a framework of critical steps to handle a situation of change. You should react according to the way you are handled. The information above is what the 'boss' thinks the real-life 'employee' *may* say. You may say something different, depending on how well you relate to the situation and how well you know the real employee.

After the practice please try to give objective feedback about how the 'boss' followed each step (see page 10), and how you felt regarding the way you were handled. Look also at page 12 and give feedback against that framework.

Thank you for helping the 'boss' to enhance his or her skills.

---

# Notes before, and during, the discussion

Notes remind you to cover essential points, to pick up new ones, and to handle them. And, on the follow-up date, you can recall what was said and agreed. Below are the notes made by the boss before, and then during, the first demonstration (about tax receipts on page 14).

His preparatory notes are shown in this type-face. He doesn't need to write much because he knows what he is talking about. Notes, including √s, made in the discussion *are in this type-face*. You can see how he carries problems from Step 4 into Step 5(a).

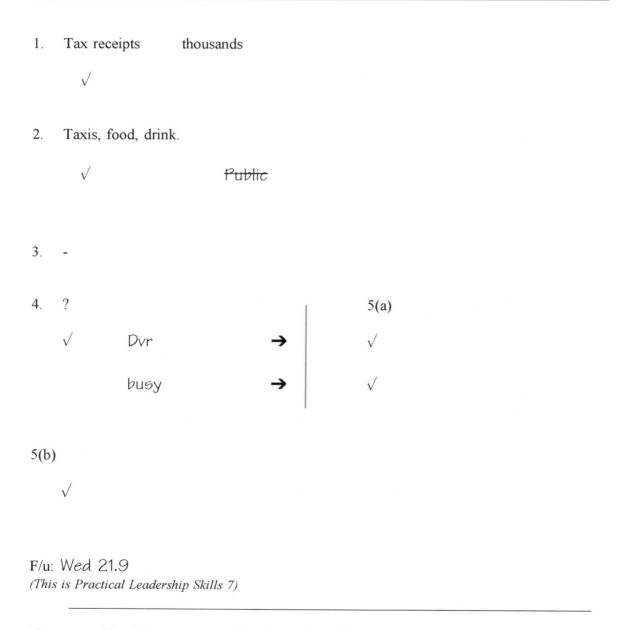

1.  Tax receipts          thousands

    √

2.  Taxis, food, drink.

    √                    ~~Public~~

3.  -

4.  ?                                         5(a)

    √        Dvr              →        √

             busy             →        √

5(b)

    √

F/u: Wed 21.9
*(This is Practical Leadership Skills 7)*

Notes on a big change, or to track a discussion with several people, would be more complex than just a few words and ticks – and you might get someone else to make them for you.

# SUMMARY

You will probably be involved in this type of discussion more than any other. 'Communicating for Co-operation' is therefore an alternative name for the framework of critical steps. The framework is a major vehicle for communication and motivation when introducing and implementing change with individuals or with groups. You have seen that each step is critical for an effective problem-solving discussion.

---

**OVERCOMING RESISTANCE TO CHANGE**

(Consider objective, implications, alternatives and discretion.)

1. Explain the conditions which have brought about the need for change.

2. Explain the detail of the change and how it will affect the employee.

3. If applicable, include a practical demonstration or teach the employee how to carry out the new process.

4. Ask the employee how he feels about the proposals; identify his major hang-ups and recognize any new problems.

5. Ask for his suggestions for

    (a) overcoming the problems and

    (b) implementing the change,

    using a joint problem-solving approach.

---

Together with Practical Leadership Skills, this framework, will help you prepare for a discussion and keep on track during it, even if it becomes difficult.

If you involve employees as early as possible you will be able to handle change relatively smoothly. If a change is modified as a result of employees' input it is more likely to be successful. But check: does it meet the original objective (or the objective as modified)?

## A word of encouragement

It is not uncommon for people to be daunted by the problems they foresee with a change, and to back away from it, or to aim for less than what is really needed. But the conditions which have brought about the need for change won't go away.

If you feel daunted go back to 'What are you trying to achieve and why?' (the objective on page 67). If change is going to be difficult, people may have to work harder at it, or smarter, or both. Or you may have to consider how the change can be broken down into smaller chunks (the incremental approach).

Either way, people will usually respond well if they understand the need for the change and are properly involved in it.

Incidentally, you will have noticed in the demonstrations that the proportion of time used in each step varied according to the situation. The same will apply to your own situations as well.

# WORKING TOWARDS A QUALIFICATION?

This book, and others in this series, will help you gain the NVQ unit in 'Managing People'. Because the book deals only with interpersonal skills, and specifically with overcoming resistance to change, it will not match all the elements in that unit.

However, this coaching style of interpersonal skills can only be used effectively if supported by knowledge of your organization's values, policies, and procedures; of the products and services you supply, your standards of service, levels of authority, etc.

## Assessment

For the assessor to decide if you meet the criteria for the NVQ unit on 'Managing People' you may:

- be asked questions on all the topics in the unit,

- be asked to simulate interactions with employees, ie giving instructions, bringing in a change, making a presentation, etc.

Other books in this series will help with further types of interactions.

Good luck!

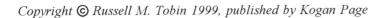

# POCKET CARD

If you would like to have a reminder to keep in your pocket, or desk drawer, or personal organizer, you can cut out the card below. Even senior managers have been known to keep the card visible when handling important discussions.

| **OVERCOMING RESISTANCE TO CHANGE** | **PRACTICAL LEADERSHIP SKILLS** |
|---|---|
| (Consider objective, implications, alternatives and discretion.) | 1. Maintain or enhance the self-esteem of the employee. |
| 1. Explain the conditions which have brought about the need for change. | 2. Don't attack the person, **focus on the problem.** |
| 2. Explain the detail of the change and how it will affect the employee. | 3. Don't assume that the employee has committed an offence. |
| 3. If applicable, include a practical demonstration or teach the employee how to carry out the new process. | 4. Encourage the employee to express his opinions and make suggestions. |
| 4. Ask the employee how he feels about the proposals; identify his major hang-ups and recognize any new problems. | 5. Allow the employee adequate time to think through the problem and suggest a solution. |
| 5. Ask for his suggestions for (a) overcoming the problems and (b) implementing the change, using a joint problem-solving approach. | 6. Ensure that the employee has an appropriate ACTION programme. |
| | 7. Always set a specific follow-up date. |
| | *Copyright © Russell M. Tobin 1999* |

# Visit Kogan Page on-line

Comprehensive information on
Kogan Page titles

## Features include

- complete catalogue listings,
  including book reviews and
  descriptions

- special monthly promotions

- information on NEW titles and
  BESTSELLING titles

- a secure shopping basket facility
  for on-line ordering

PLUS everything you need to know
about KOGAN PAGE

## http://www.kogan-page.co.uk